ISBN-13:
978-1519180445

ISBN-10:
1519180446

JUSTIN AERNI SUCKS!
Eighty Original Drawings

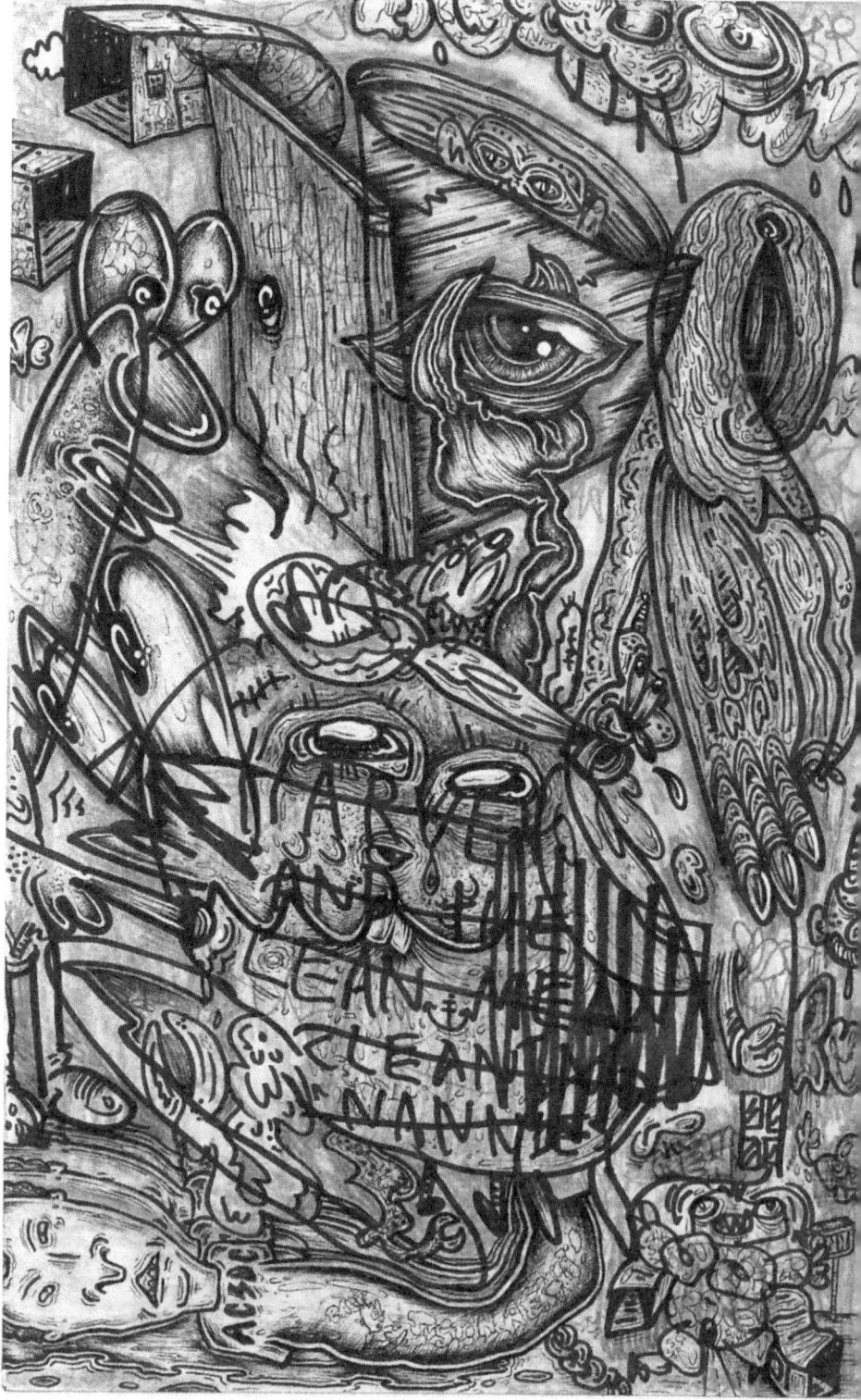

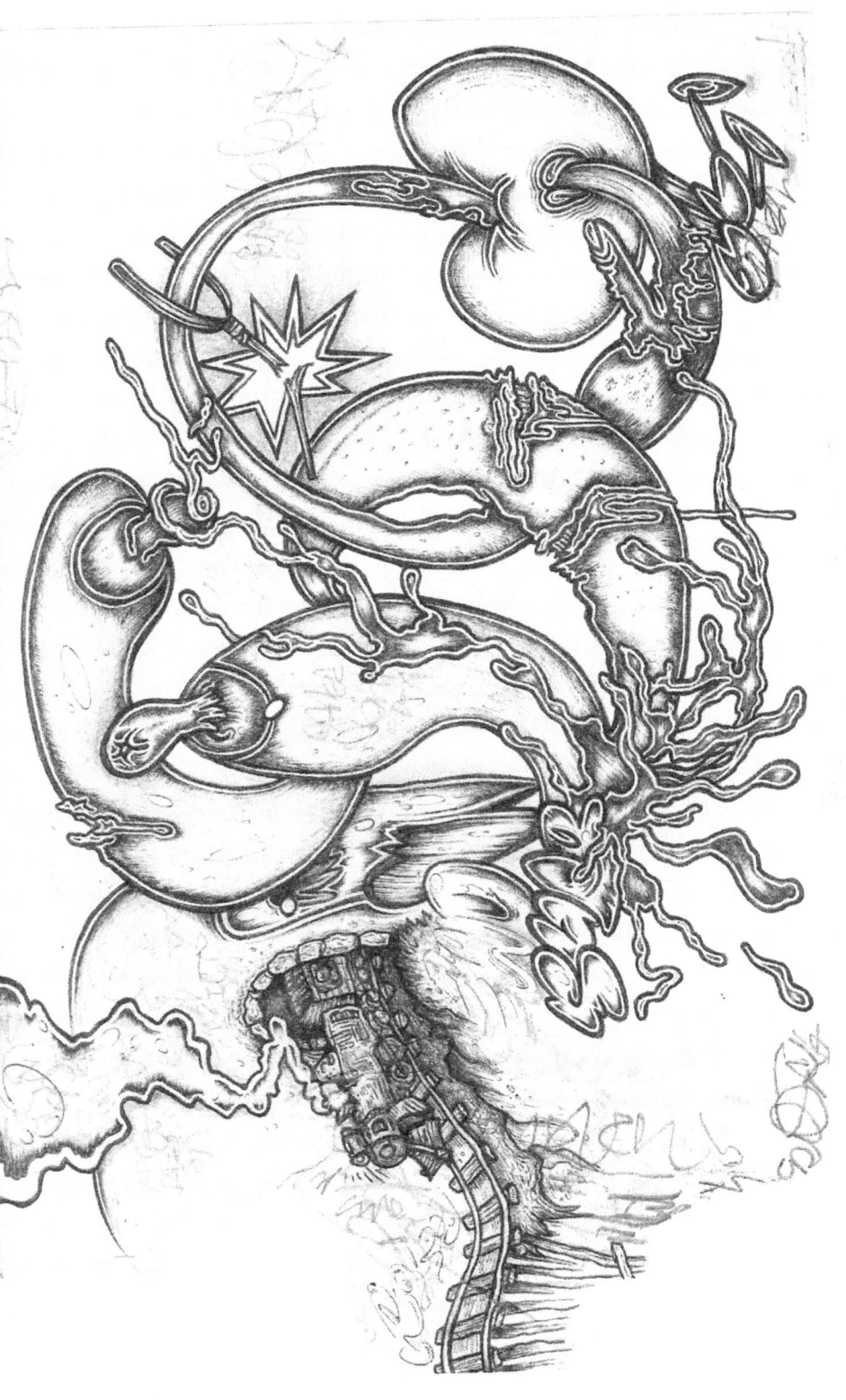

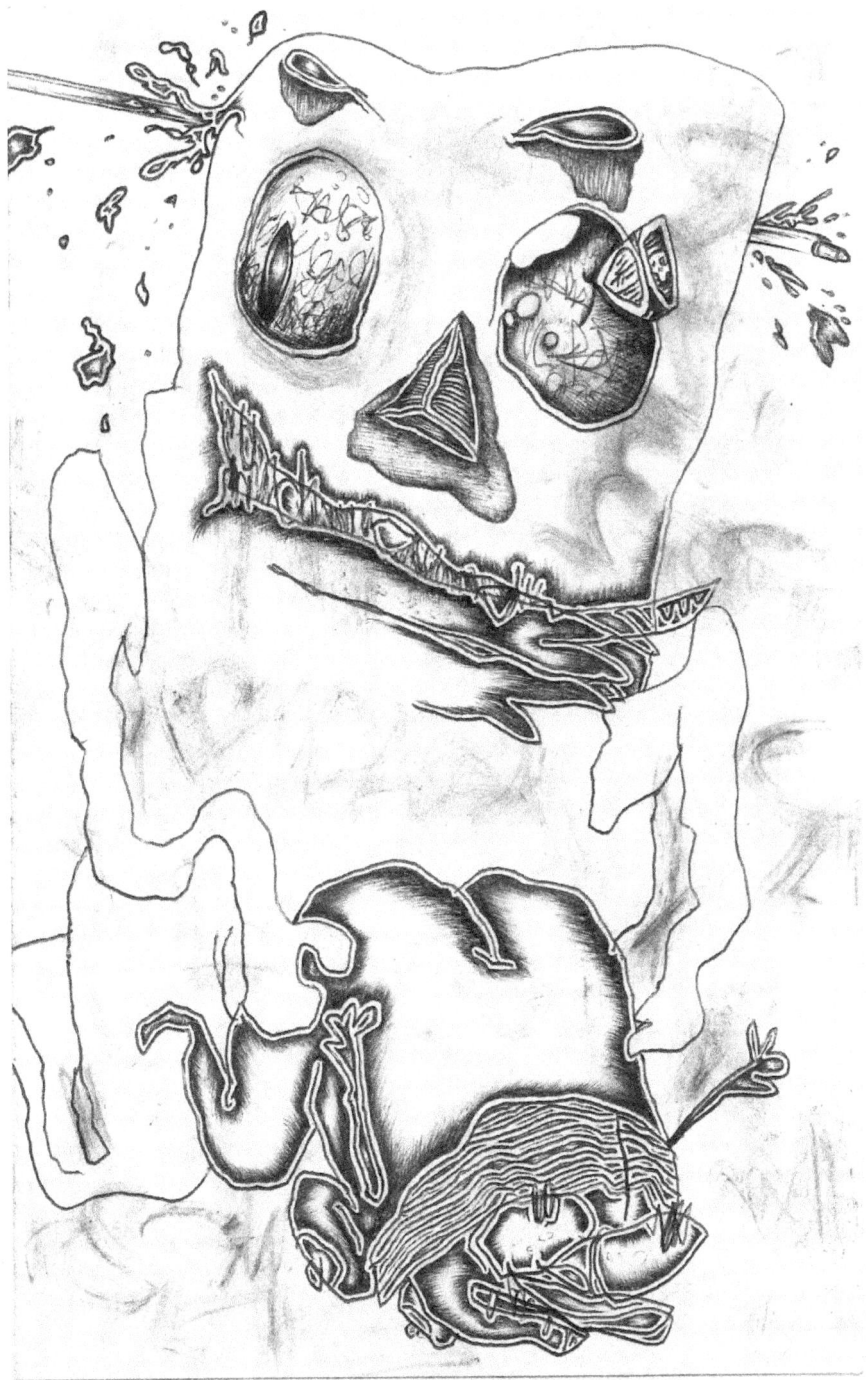

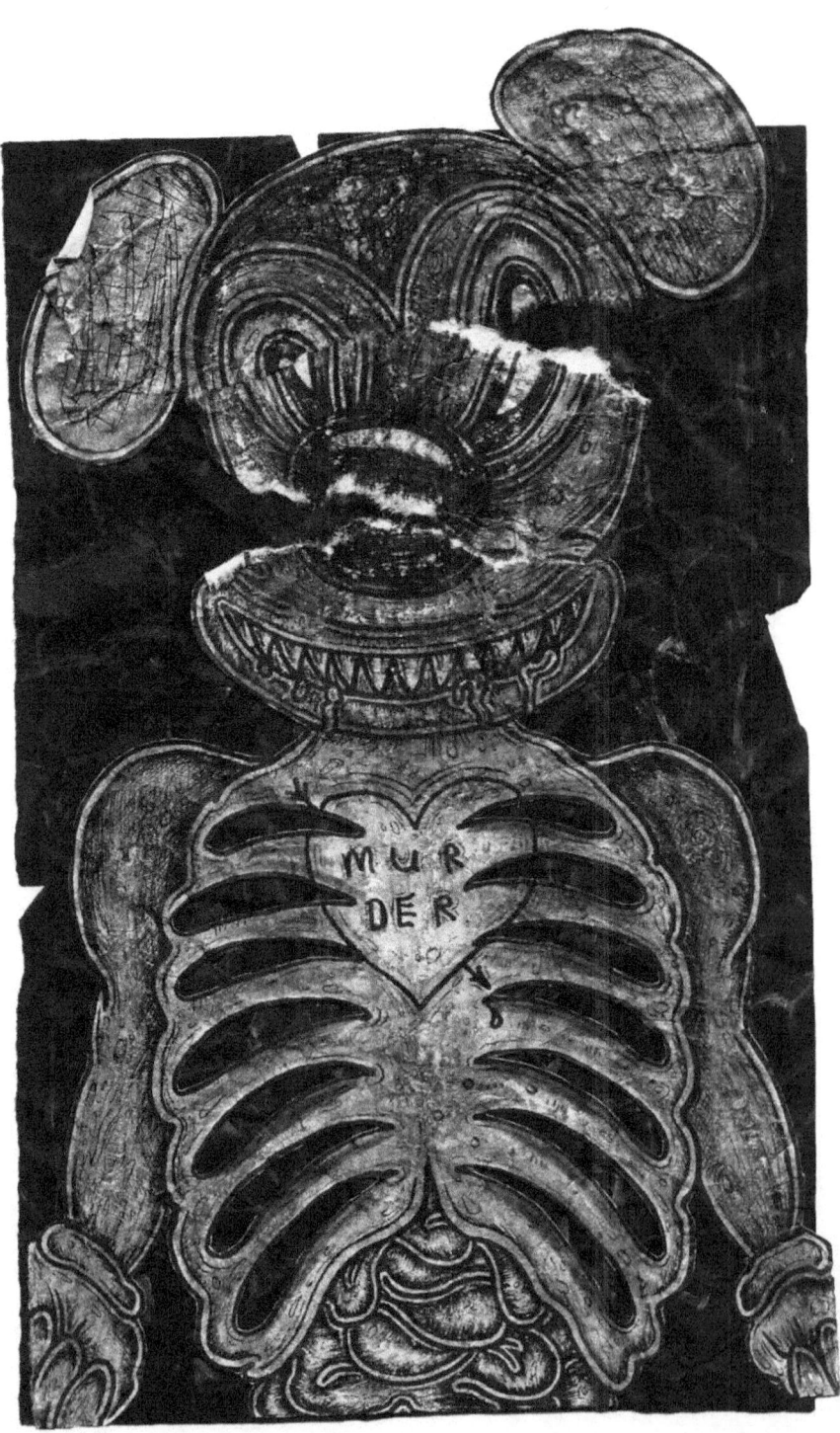

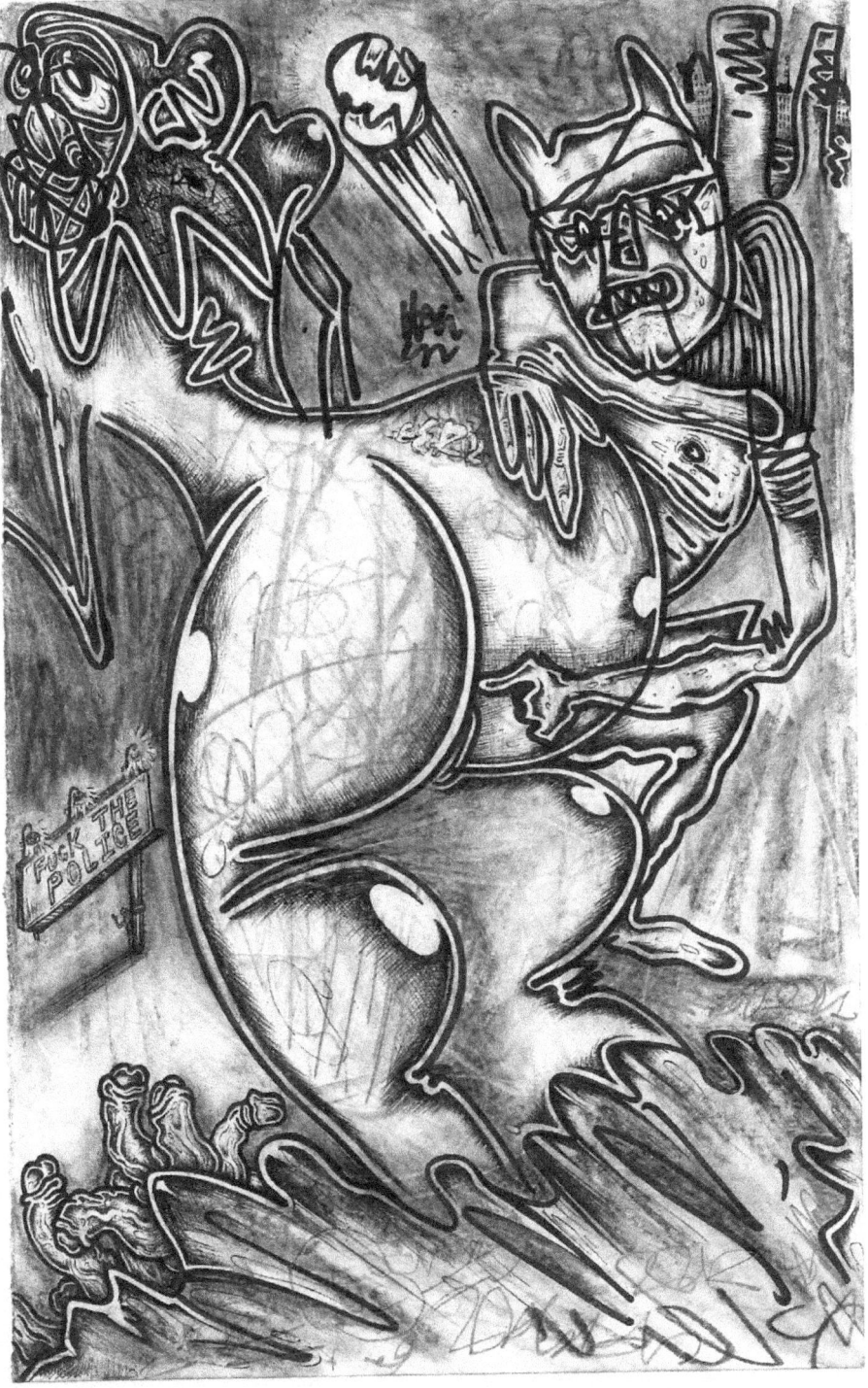

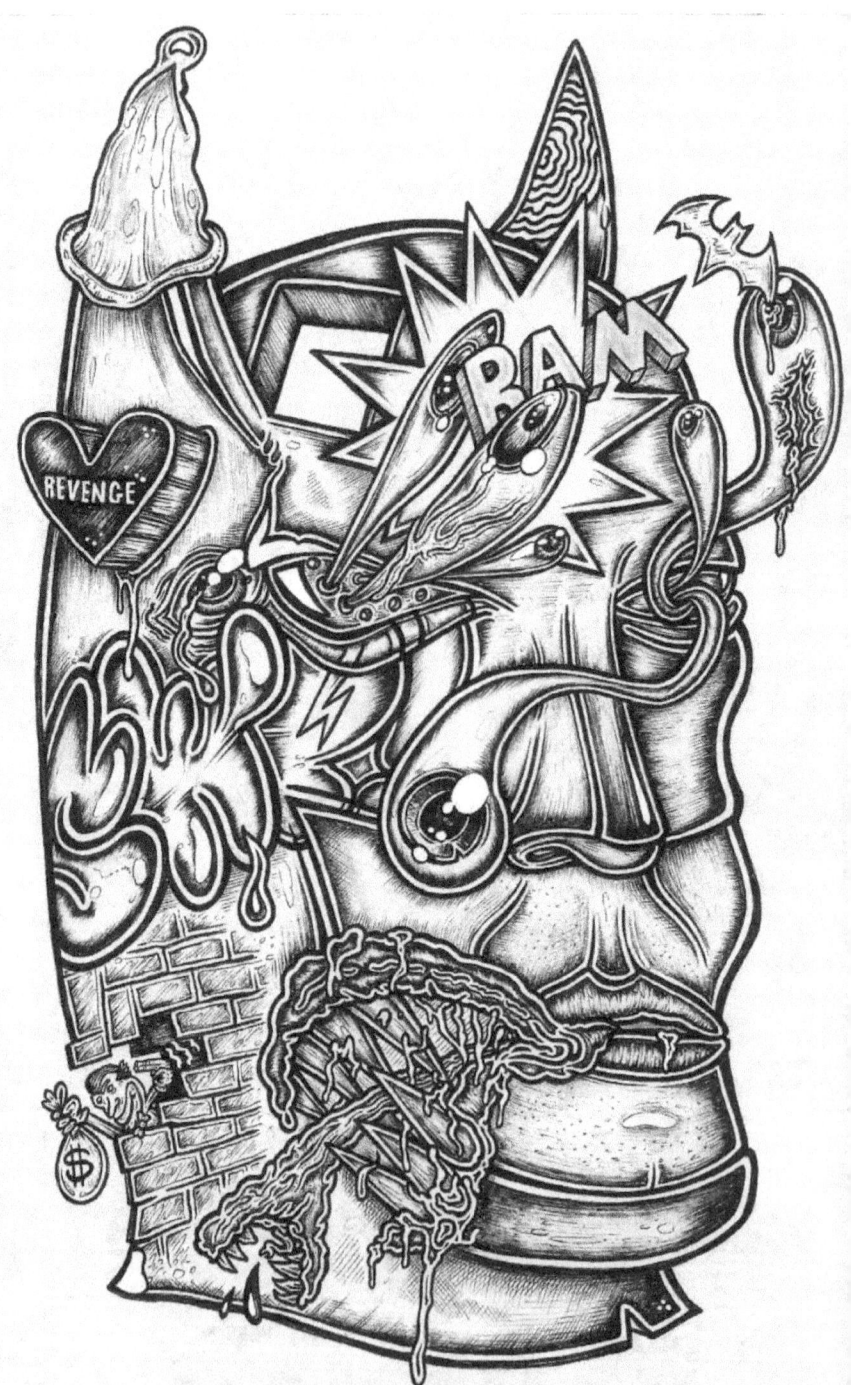

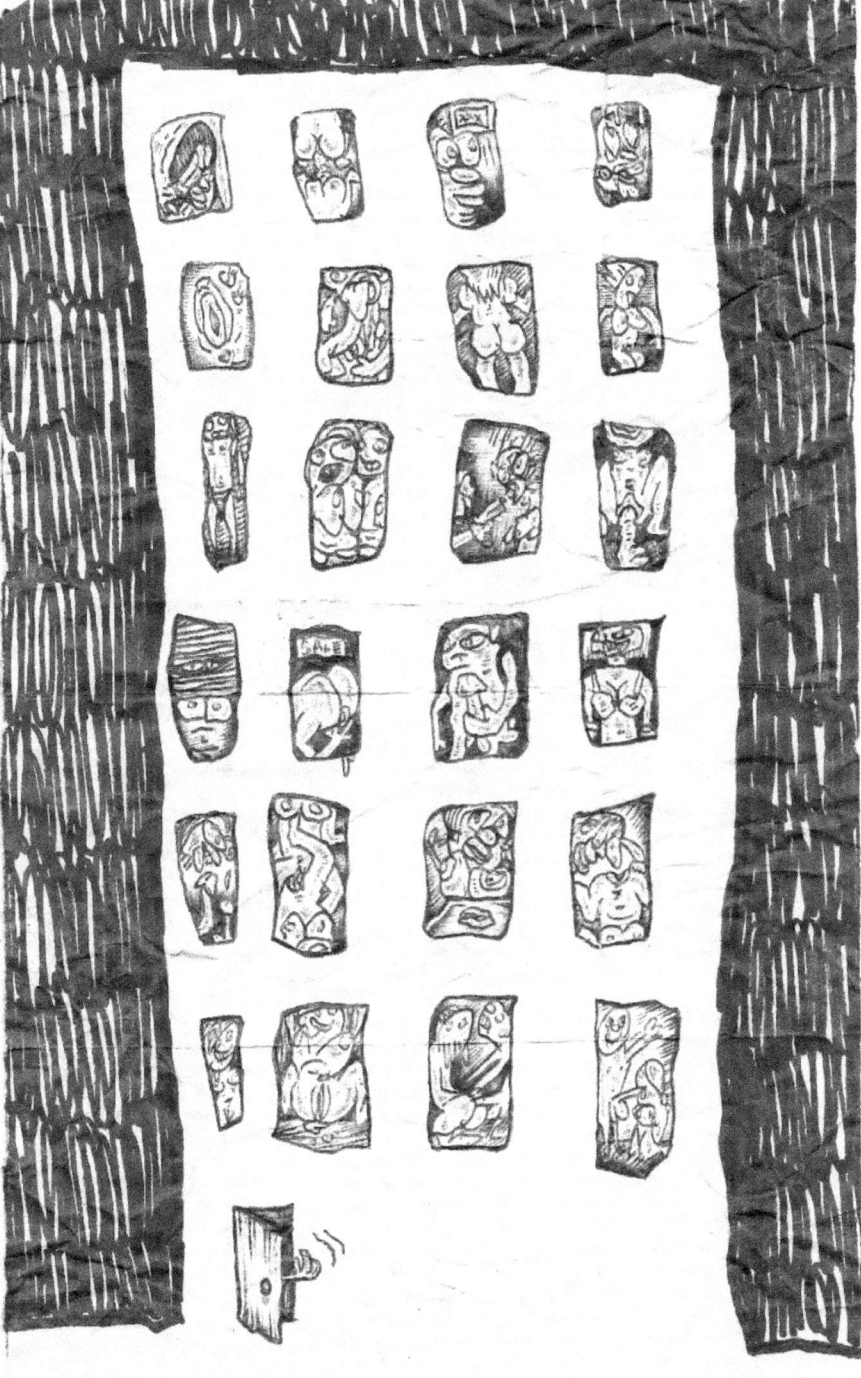

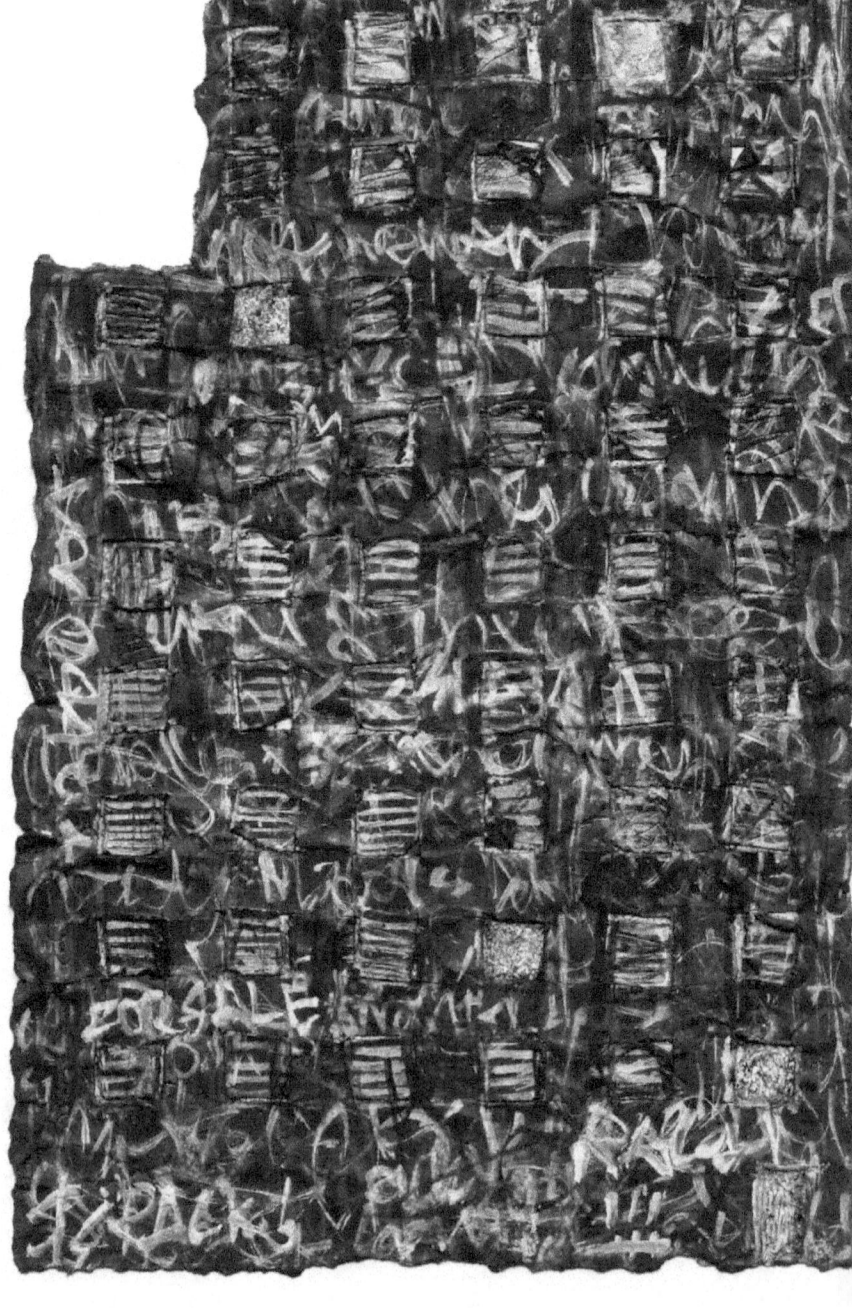

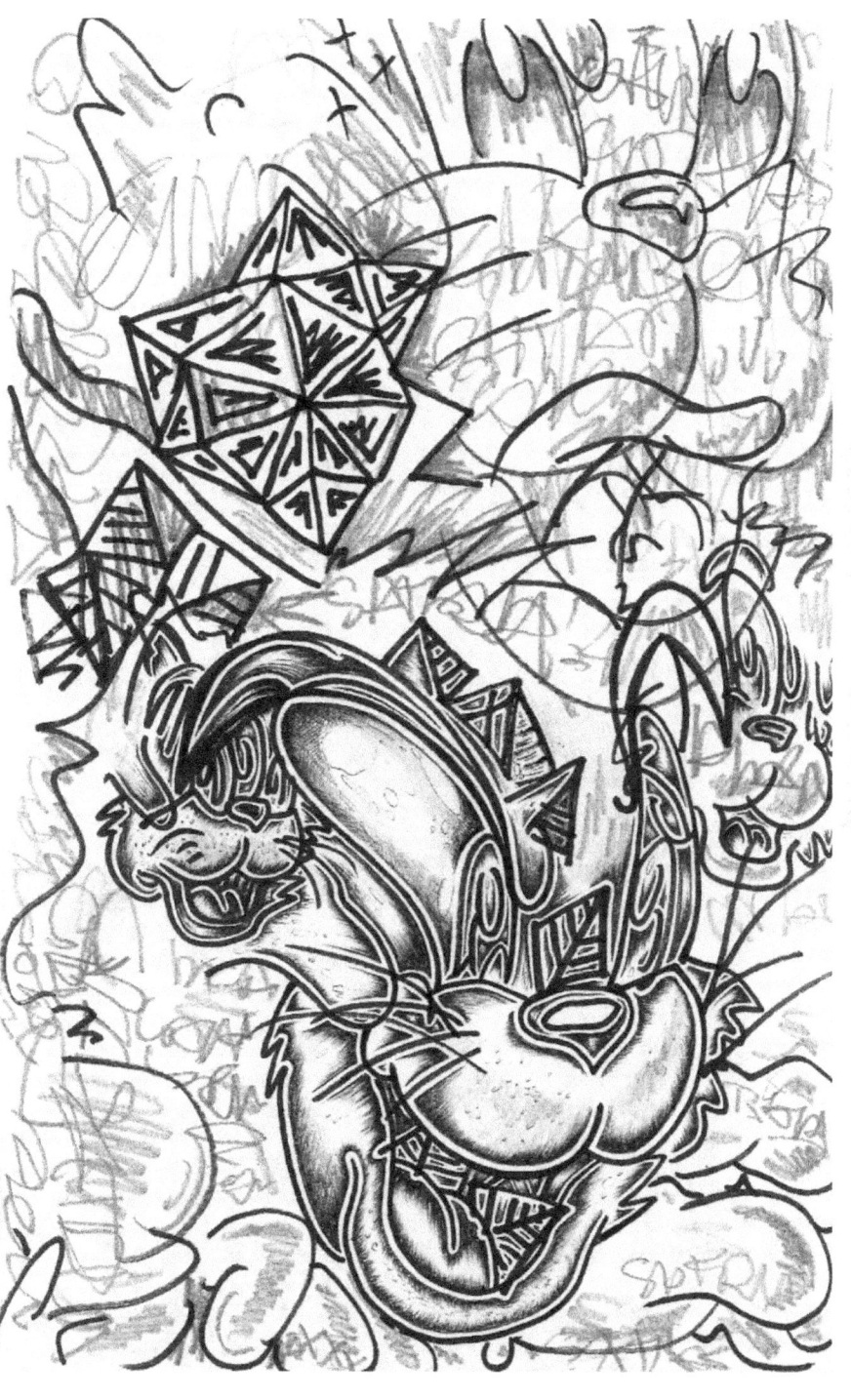

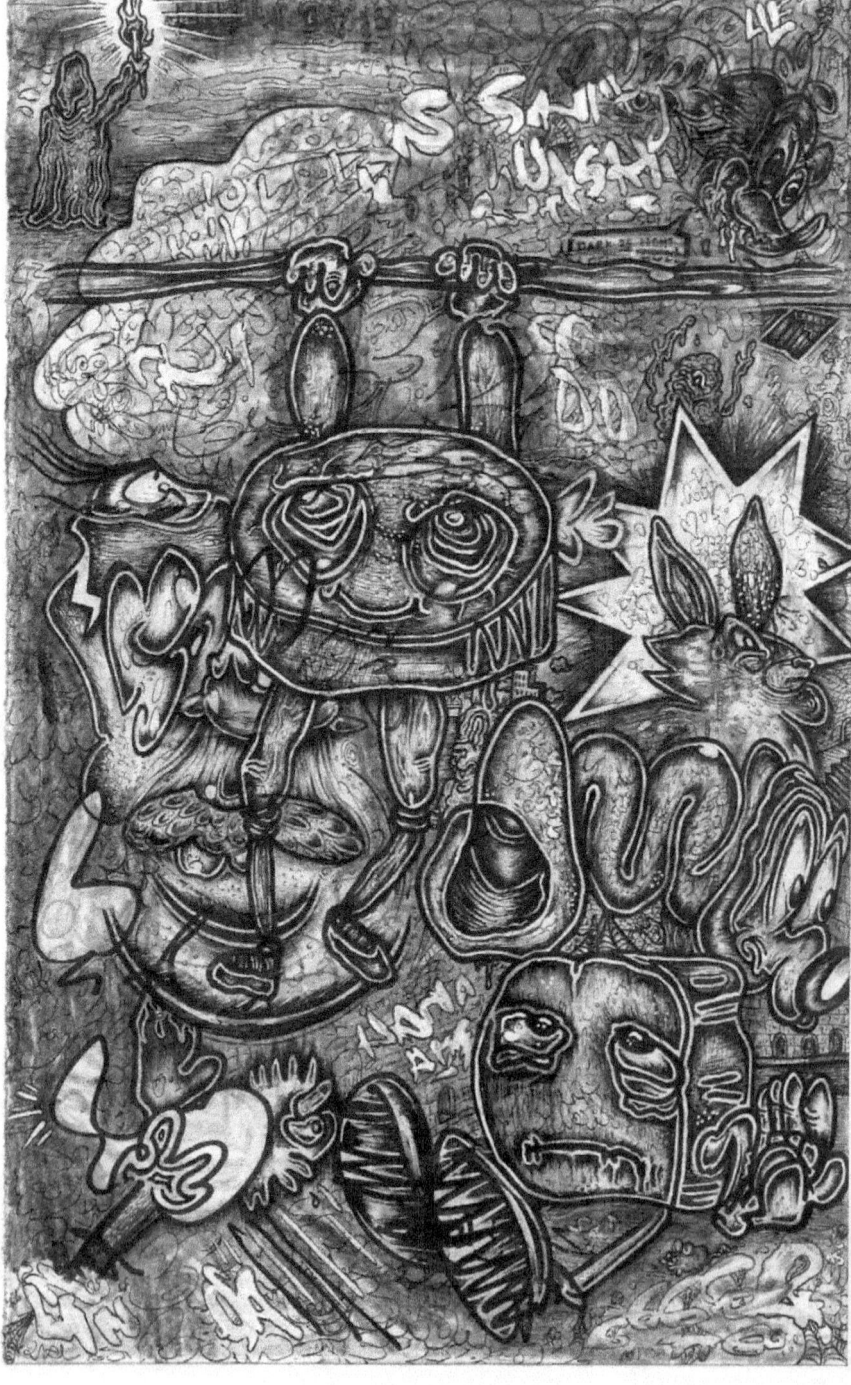

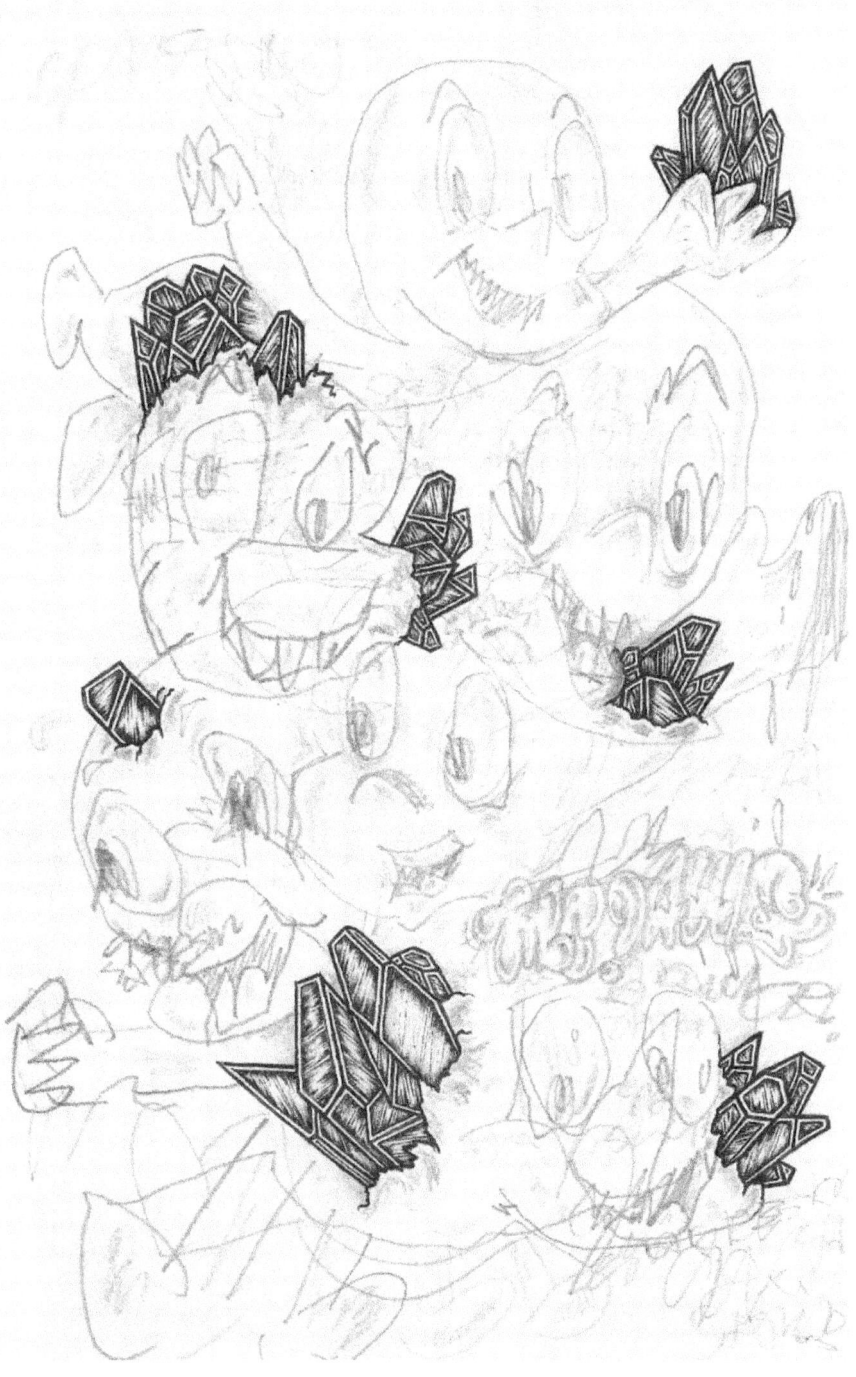

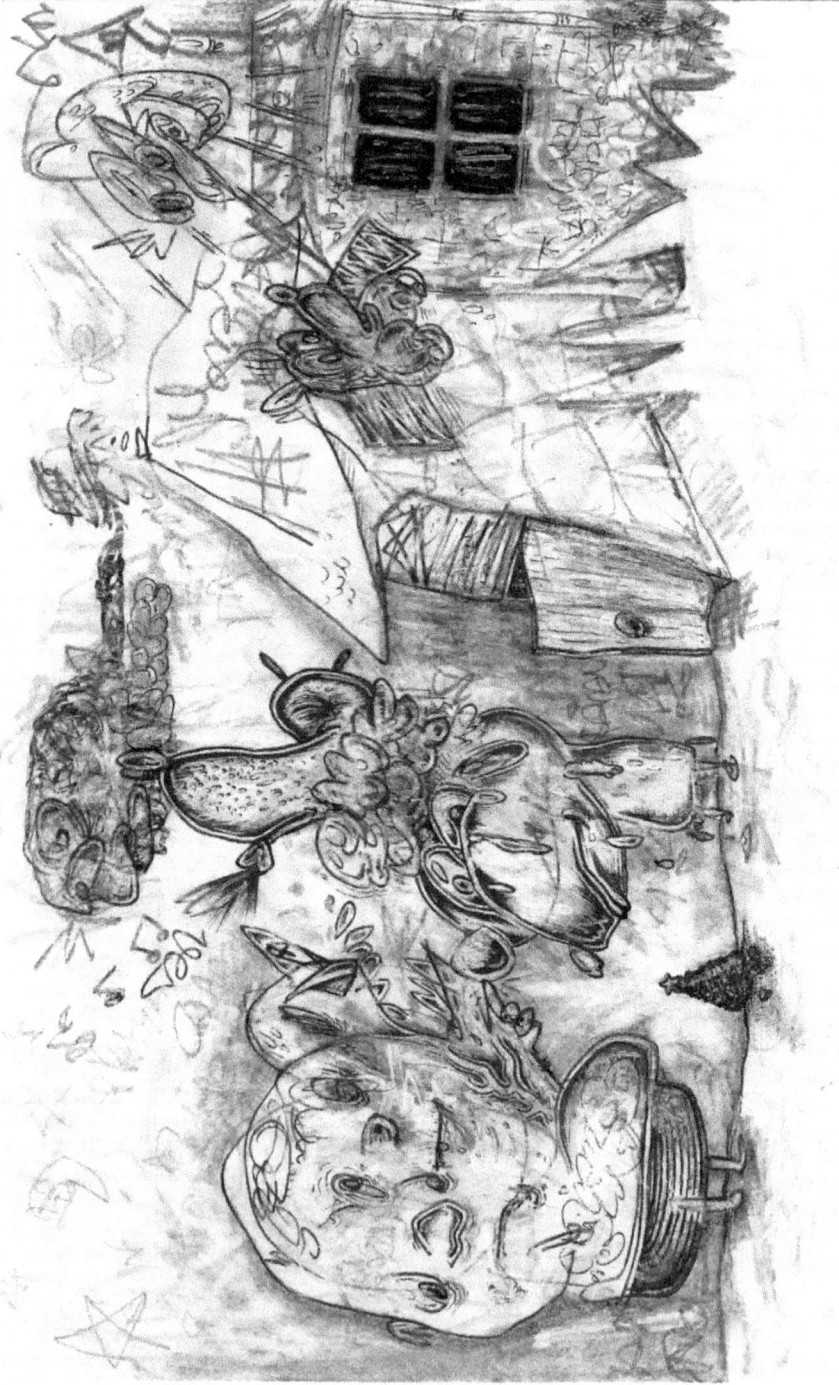

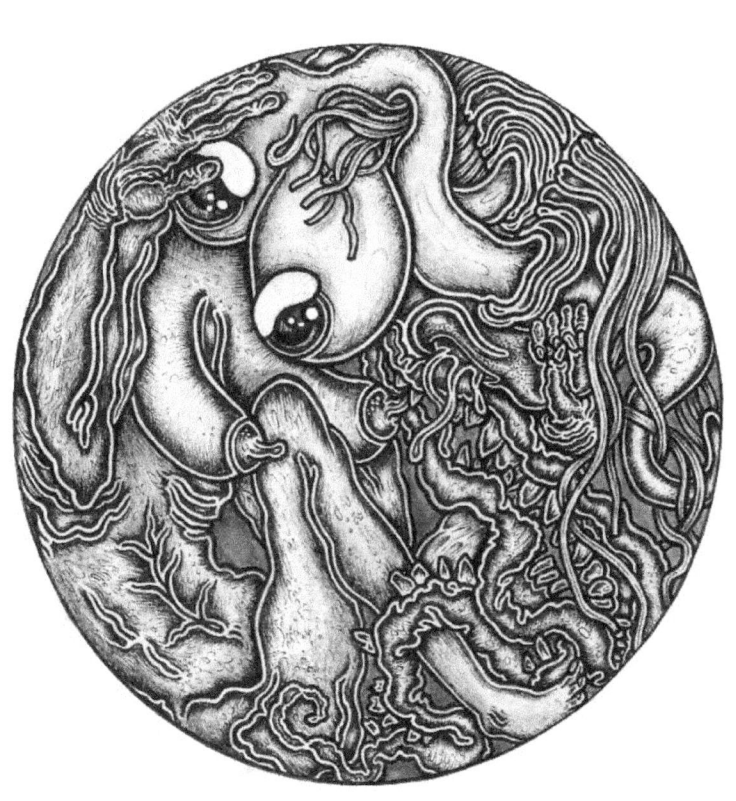

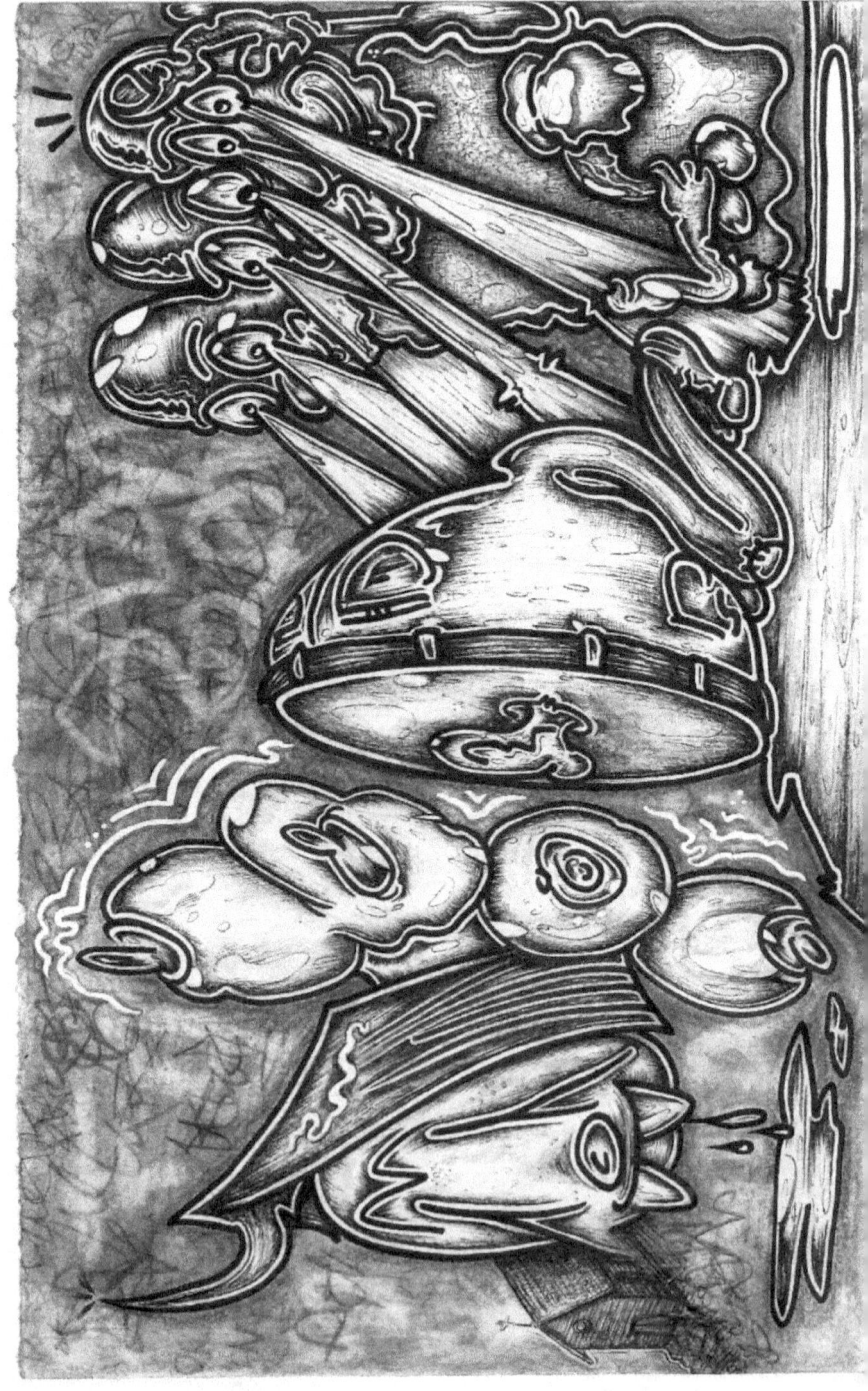

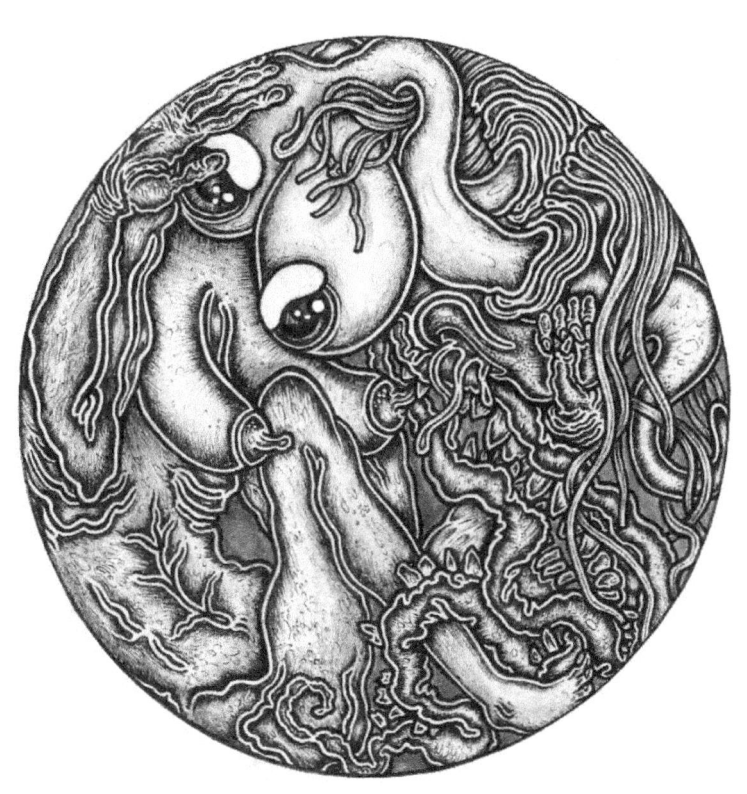

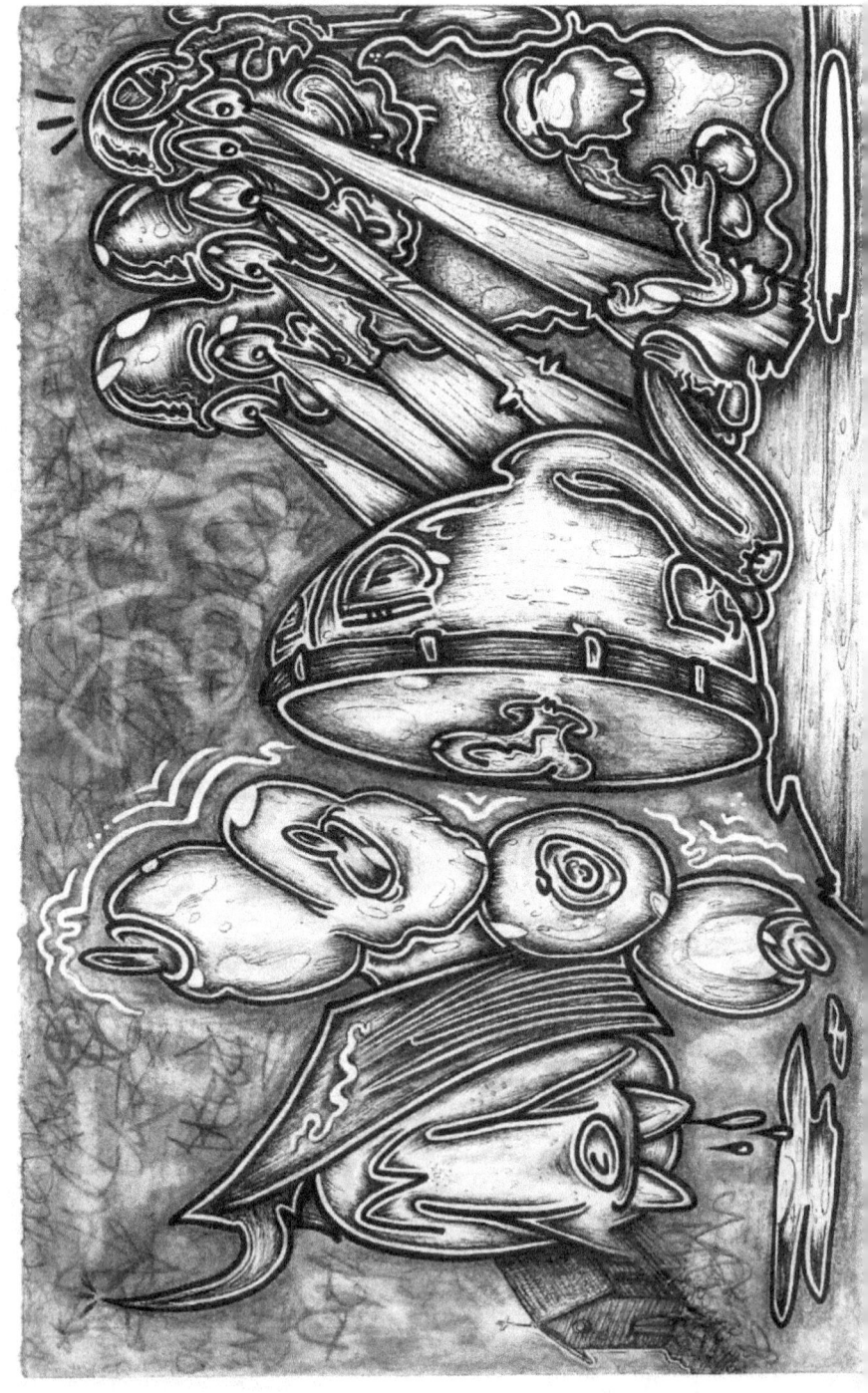

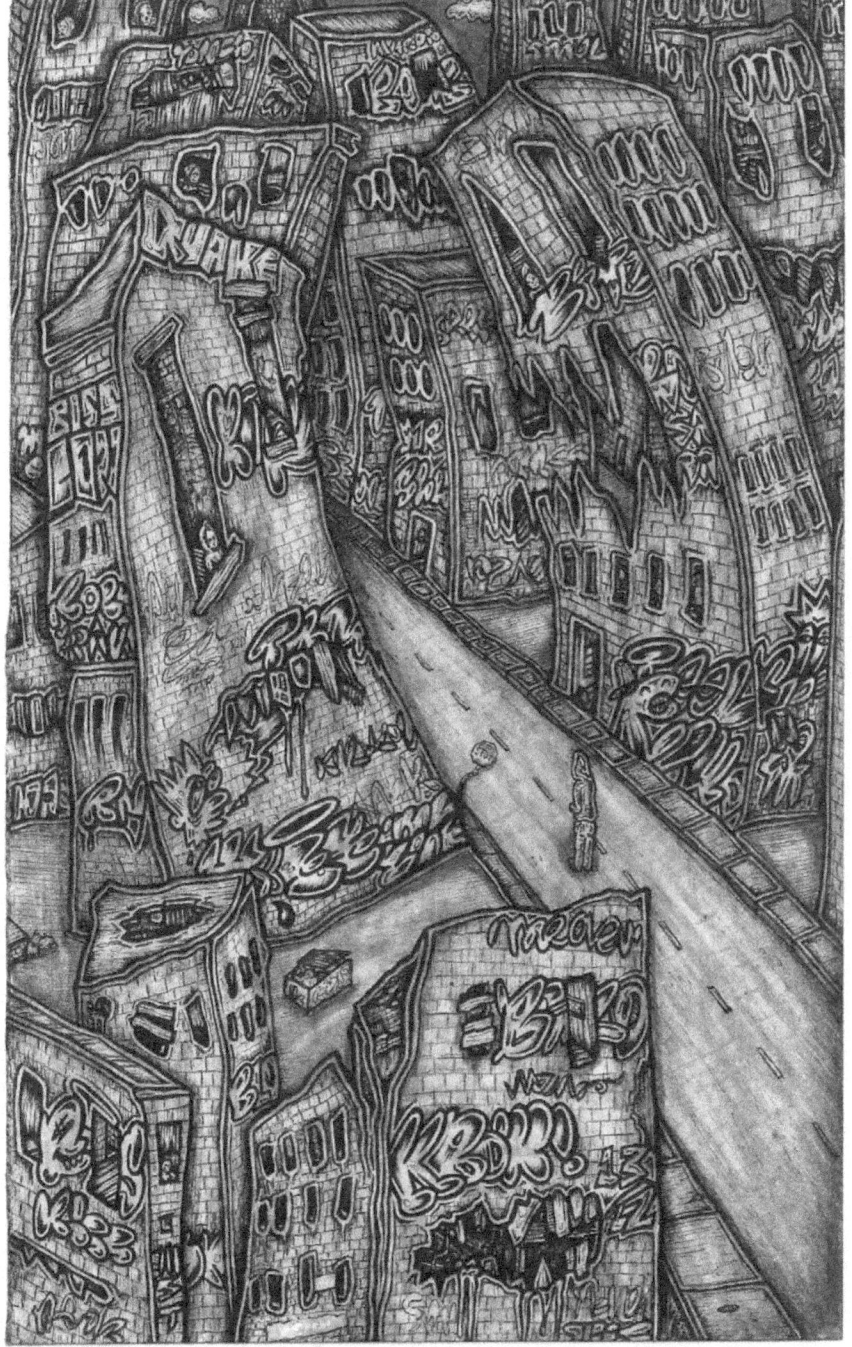

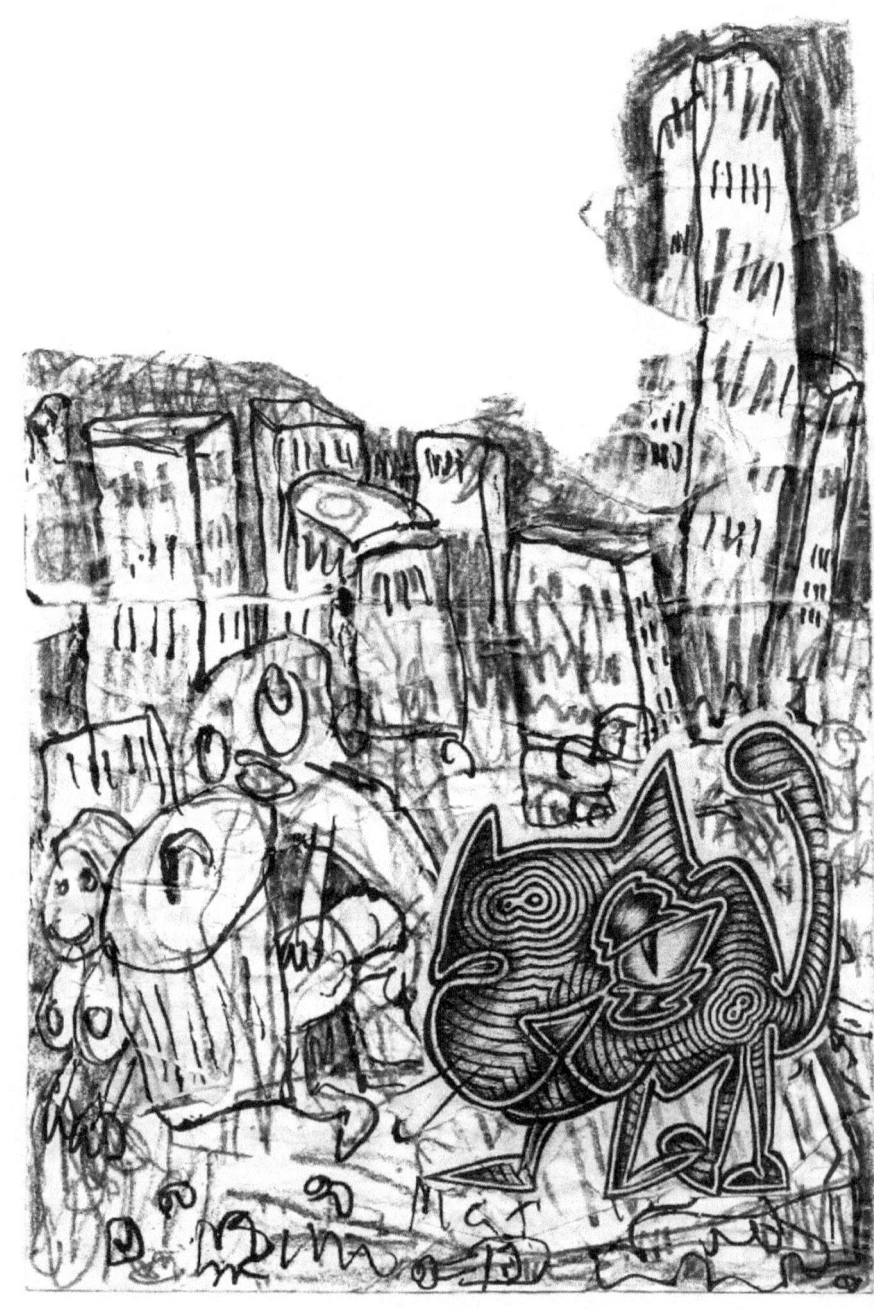

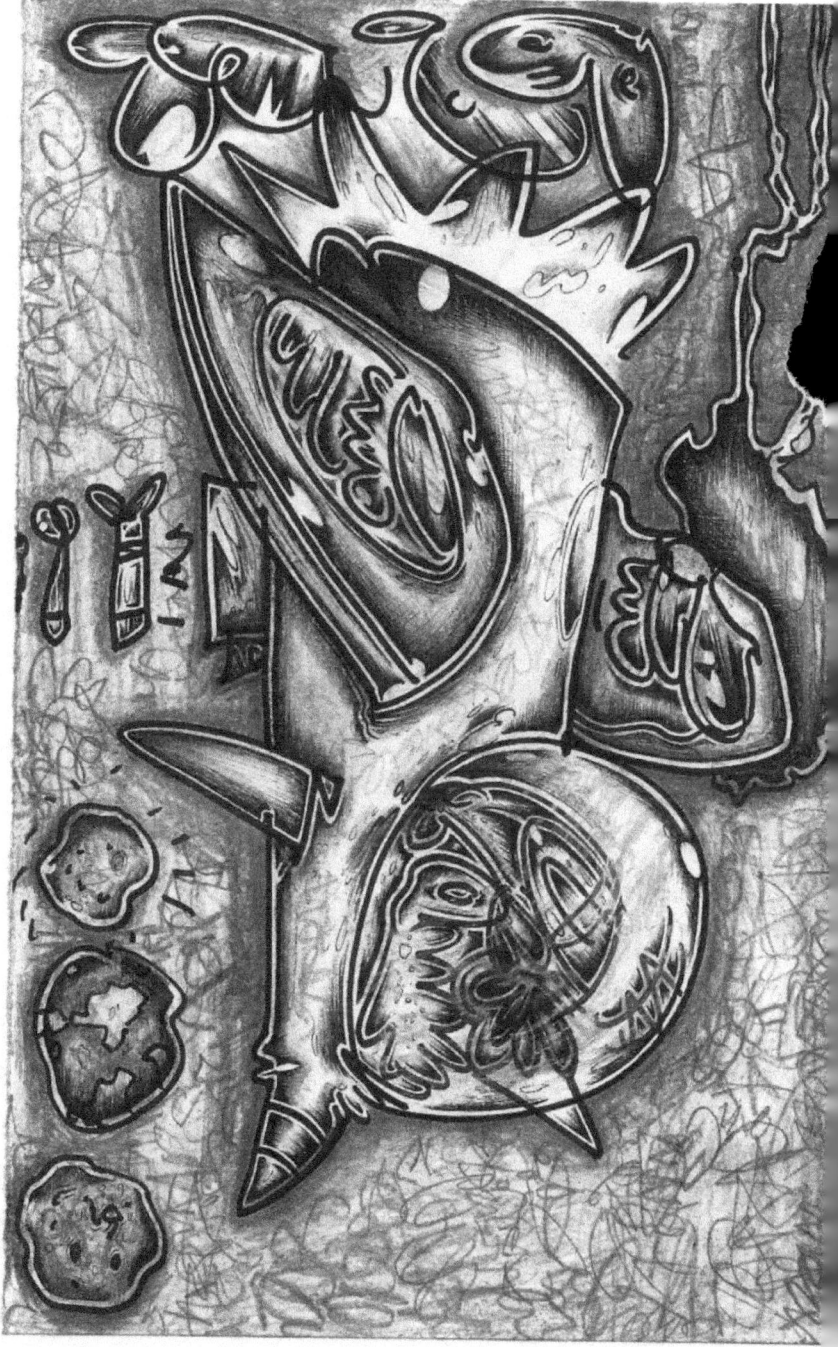

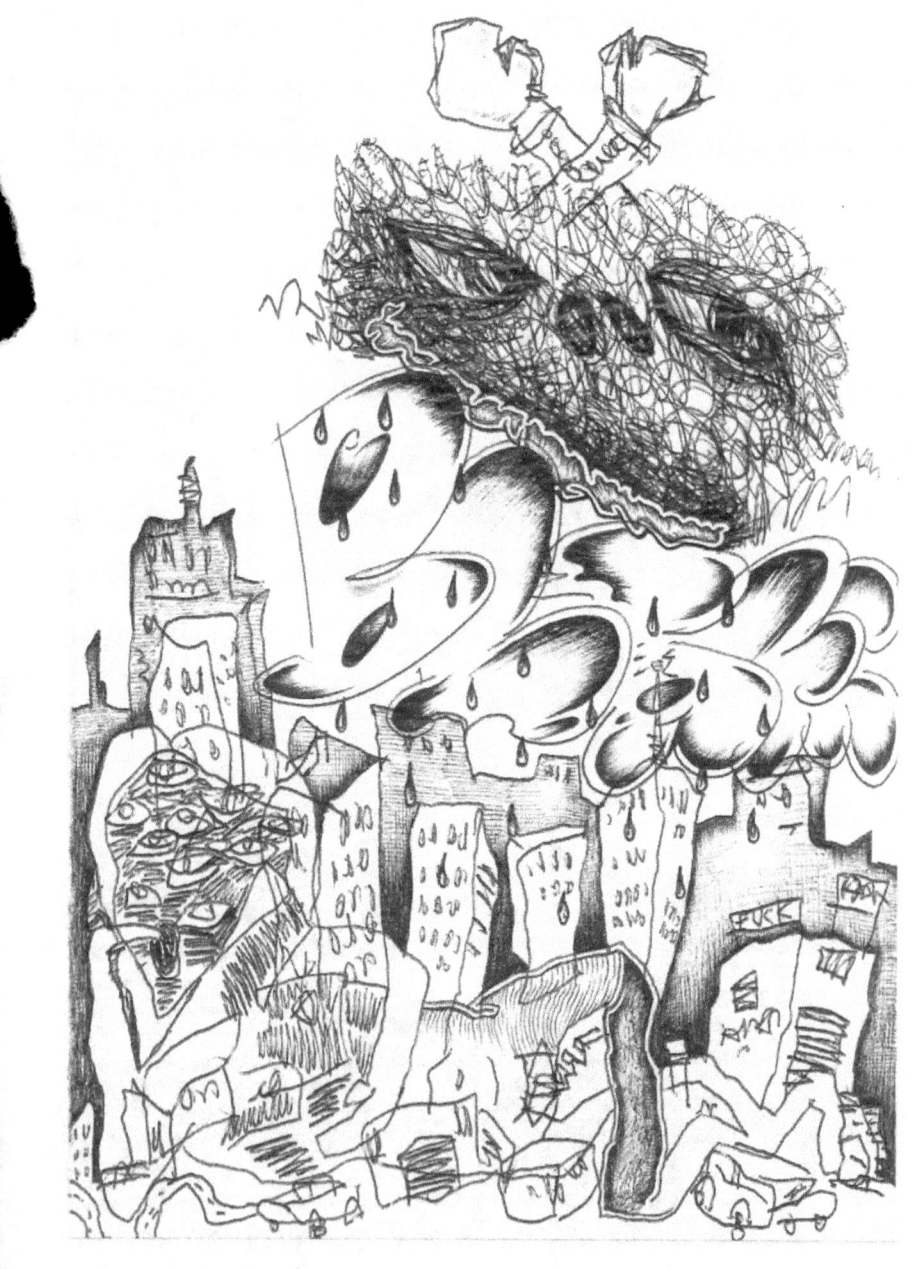

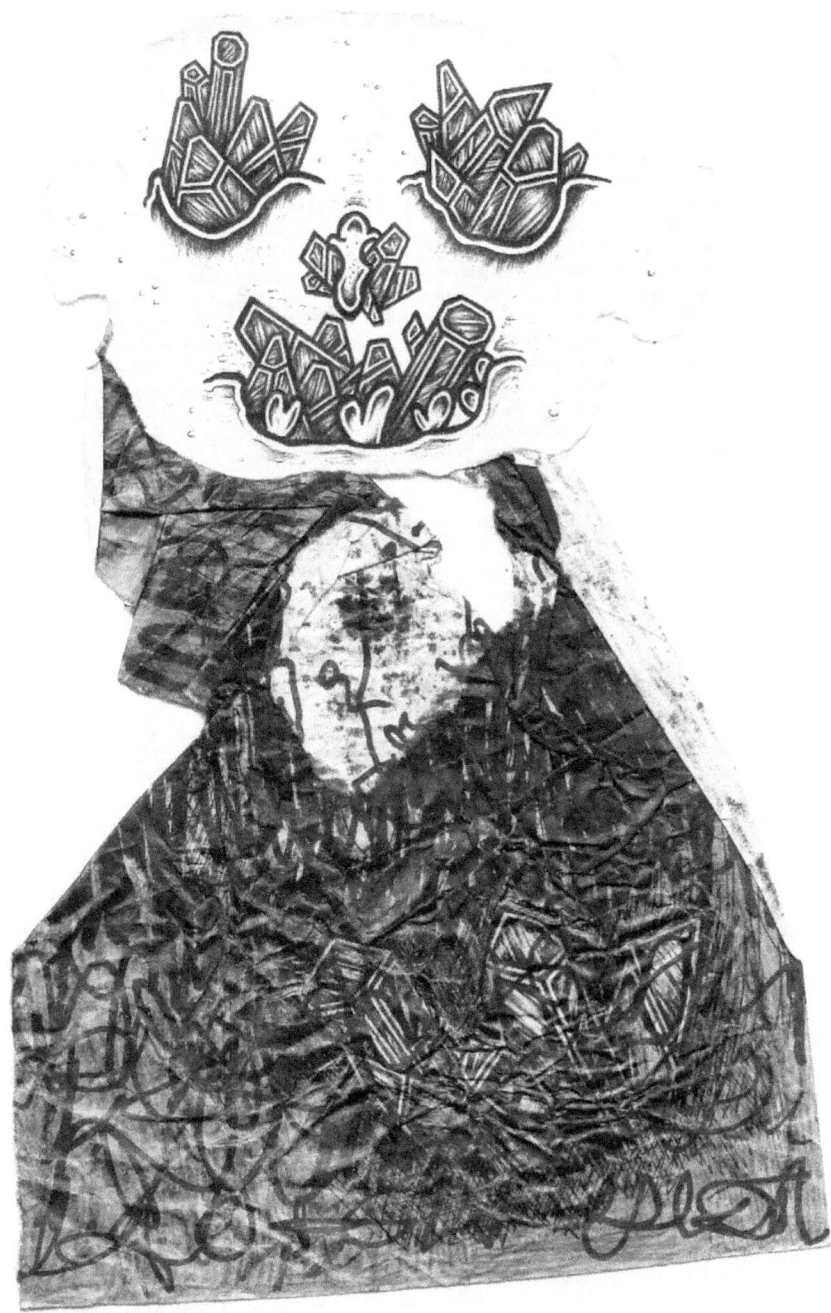

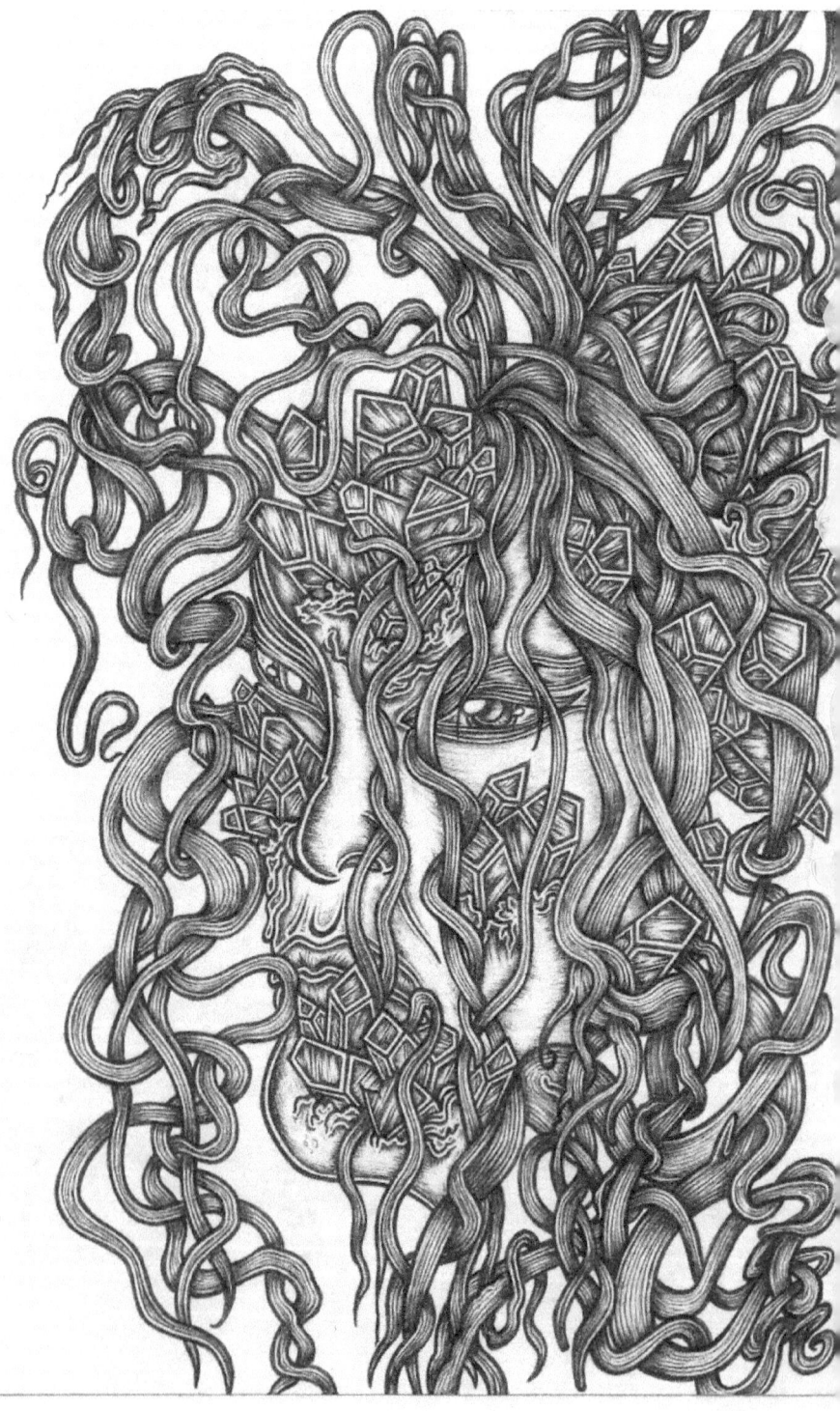

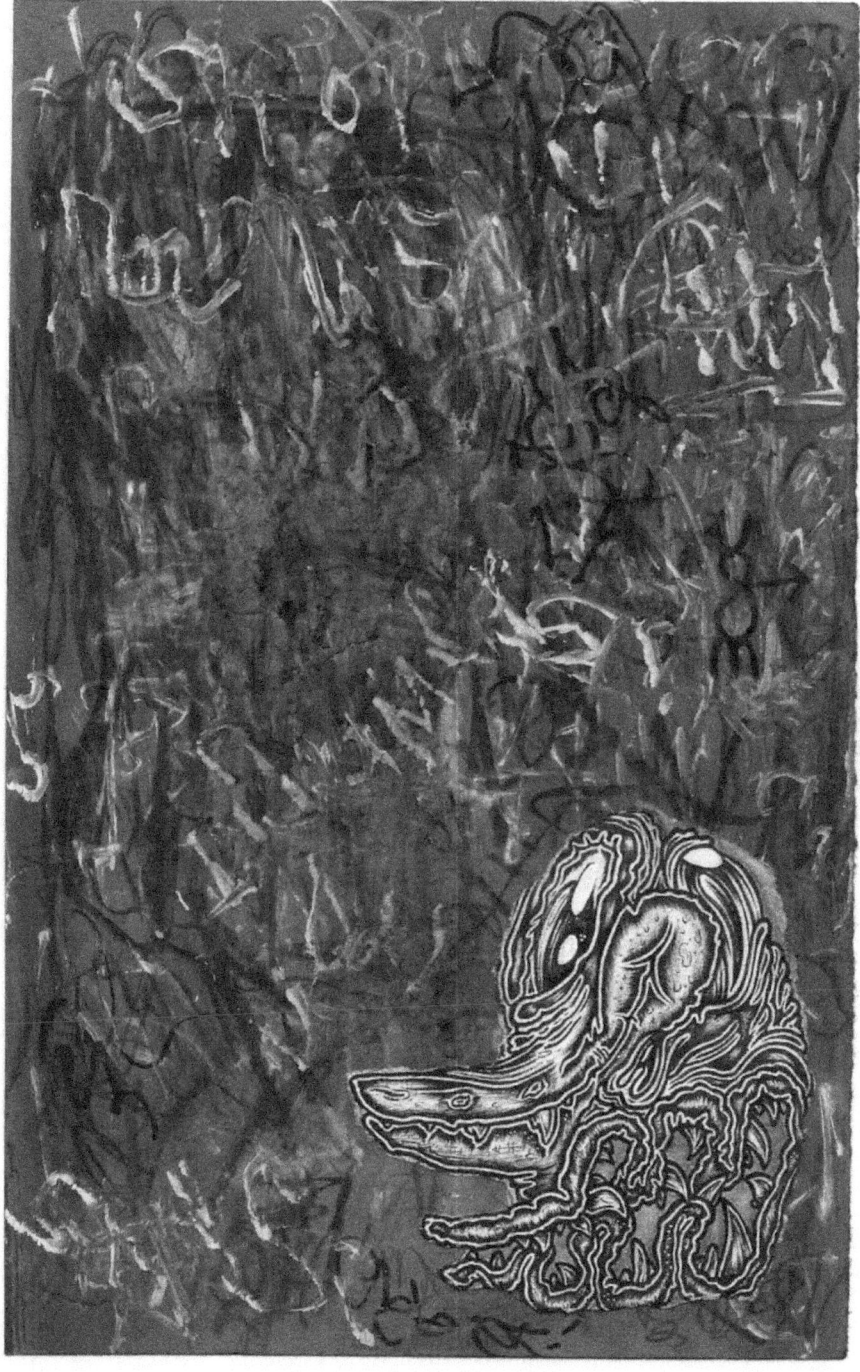

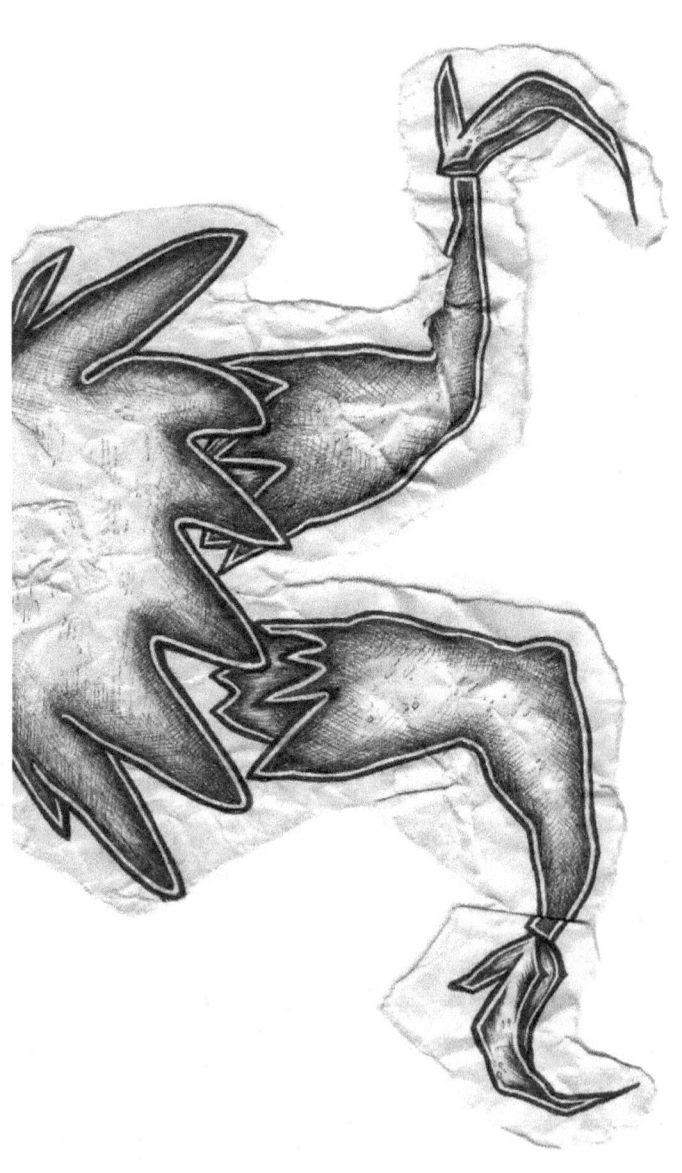

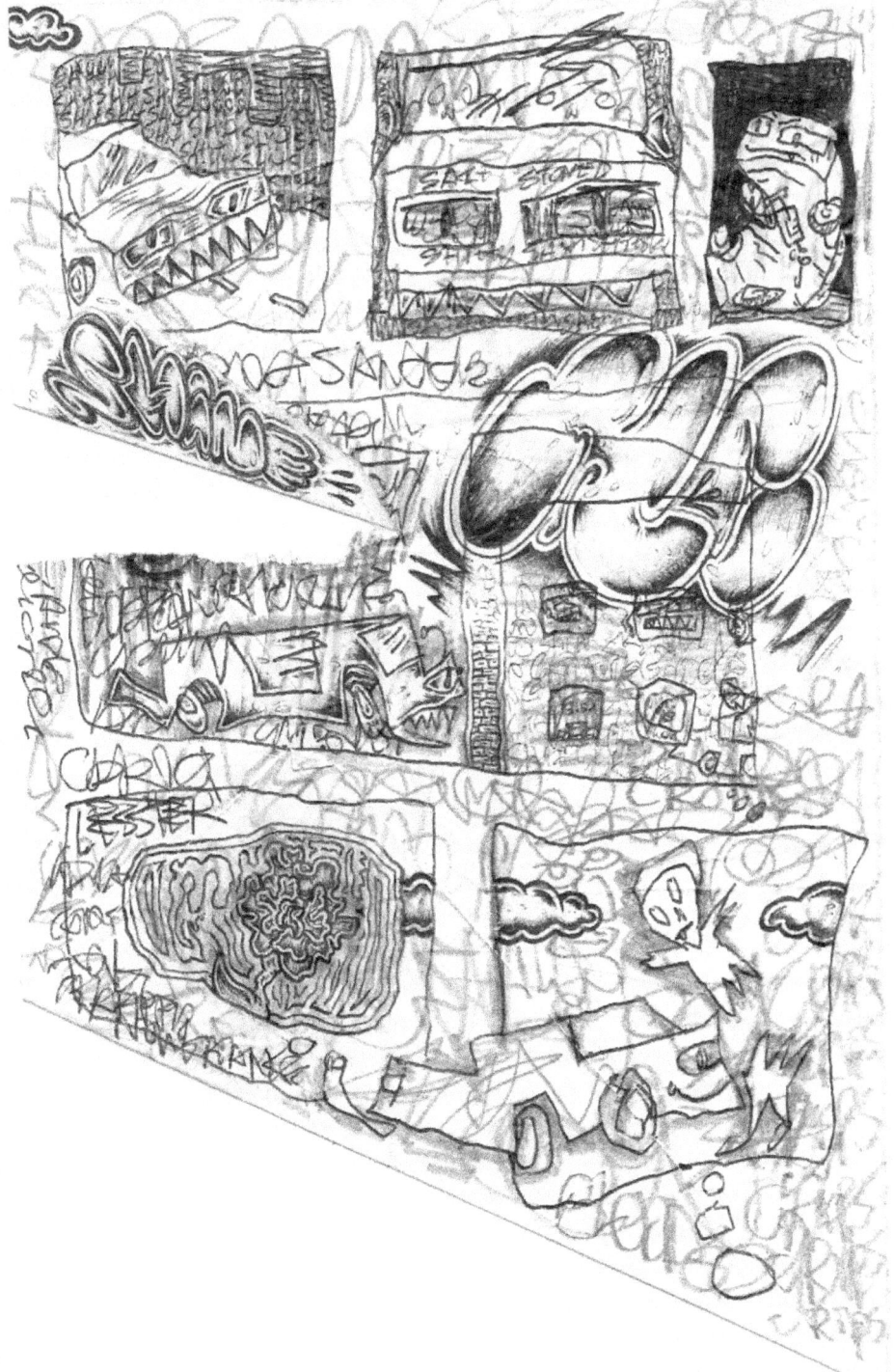

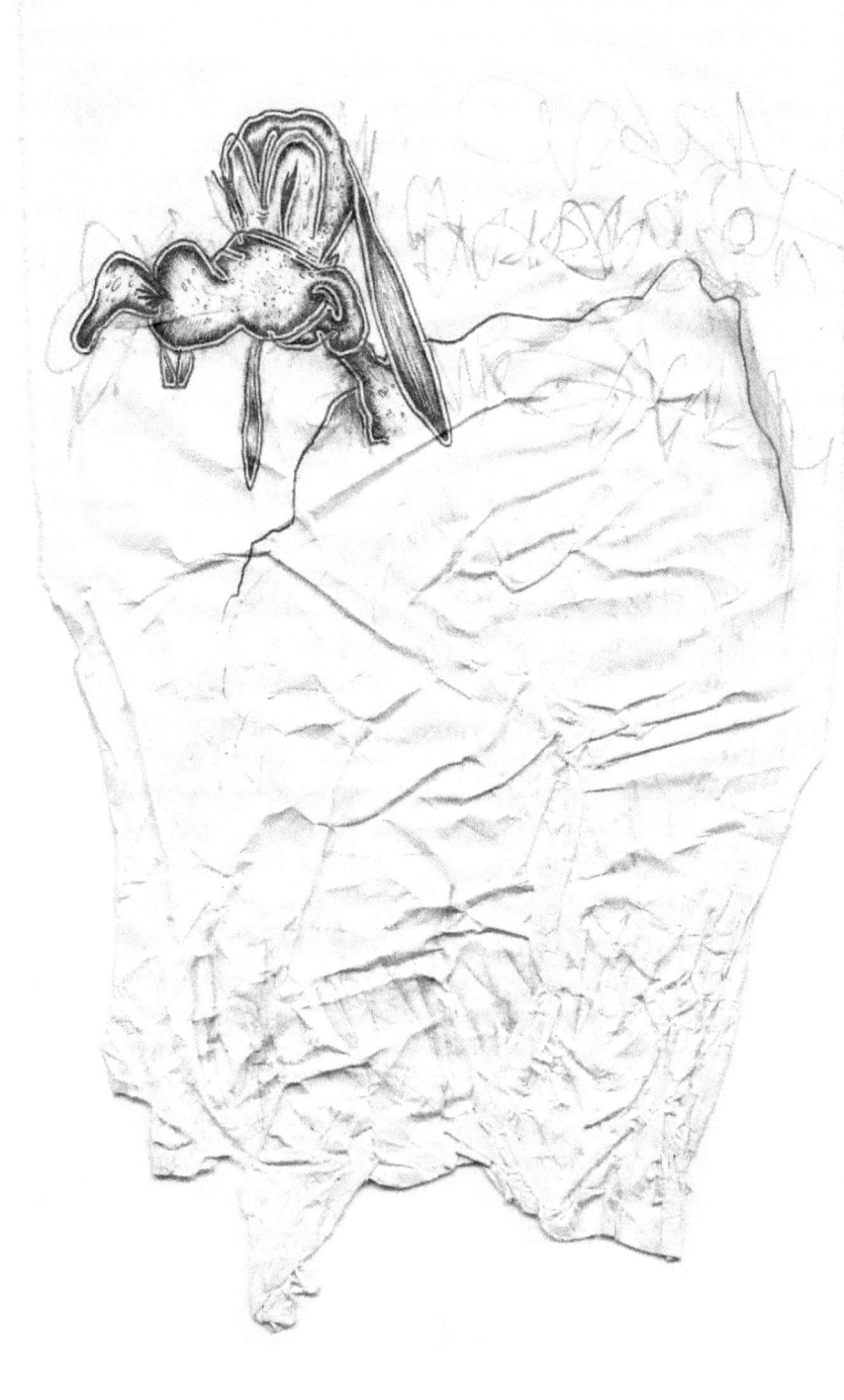

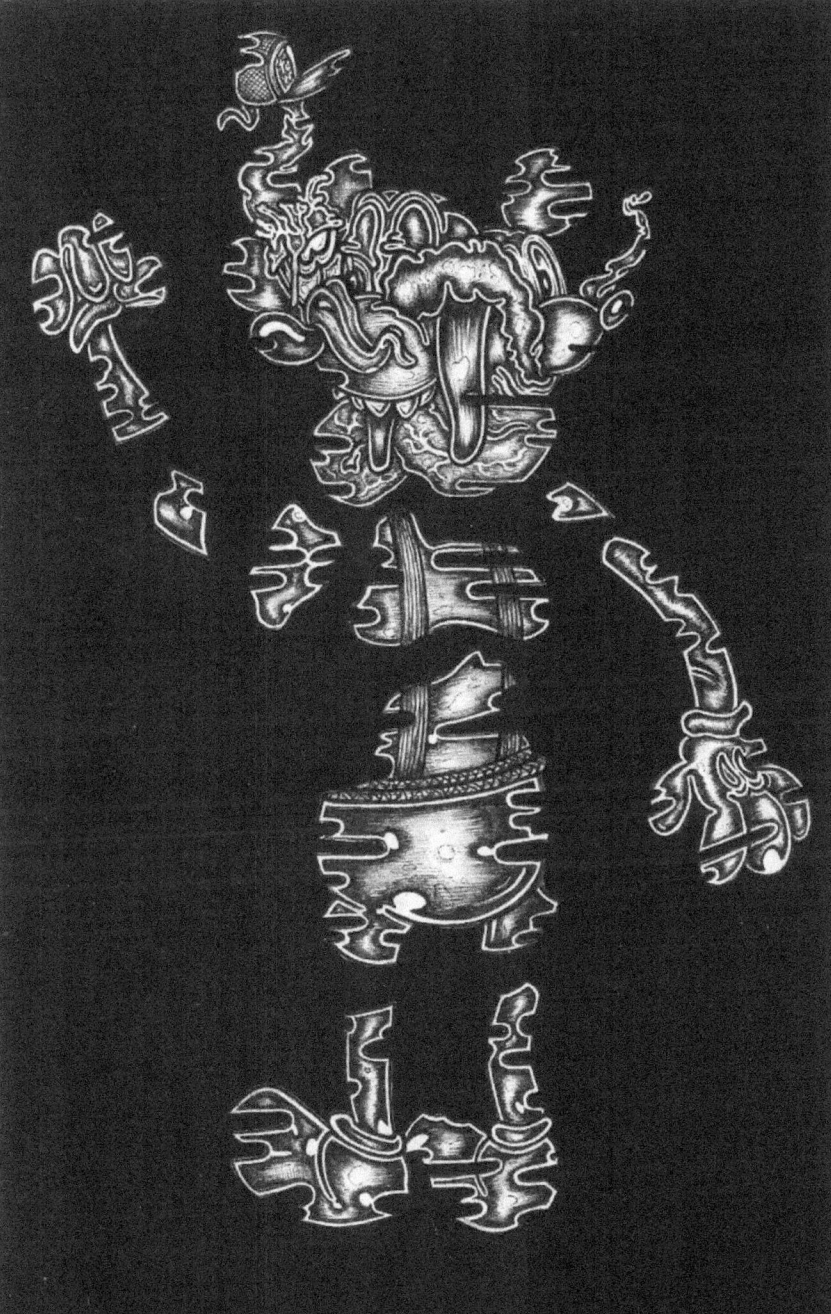

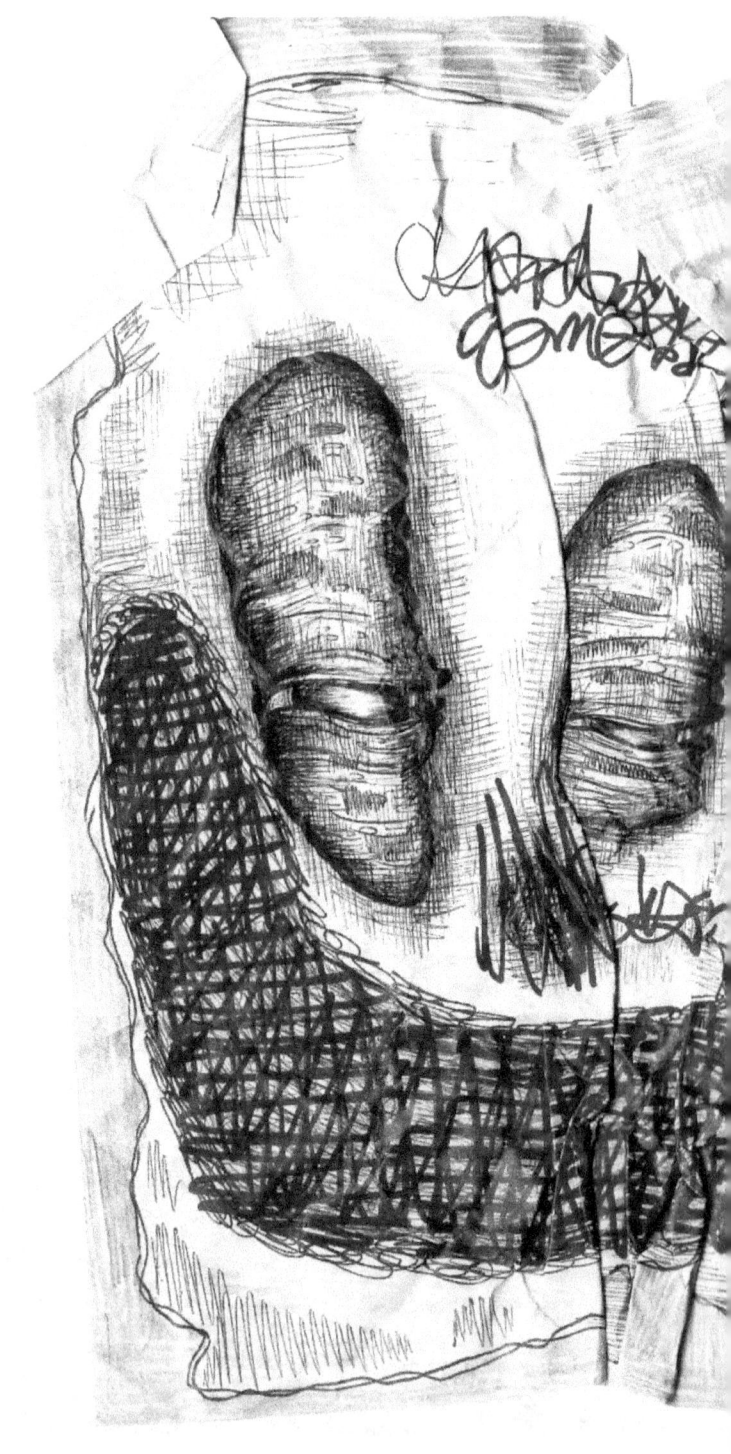

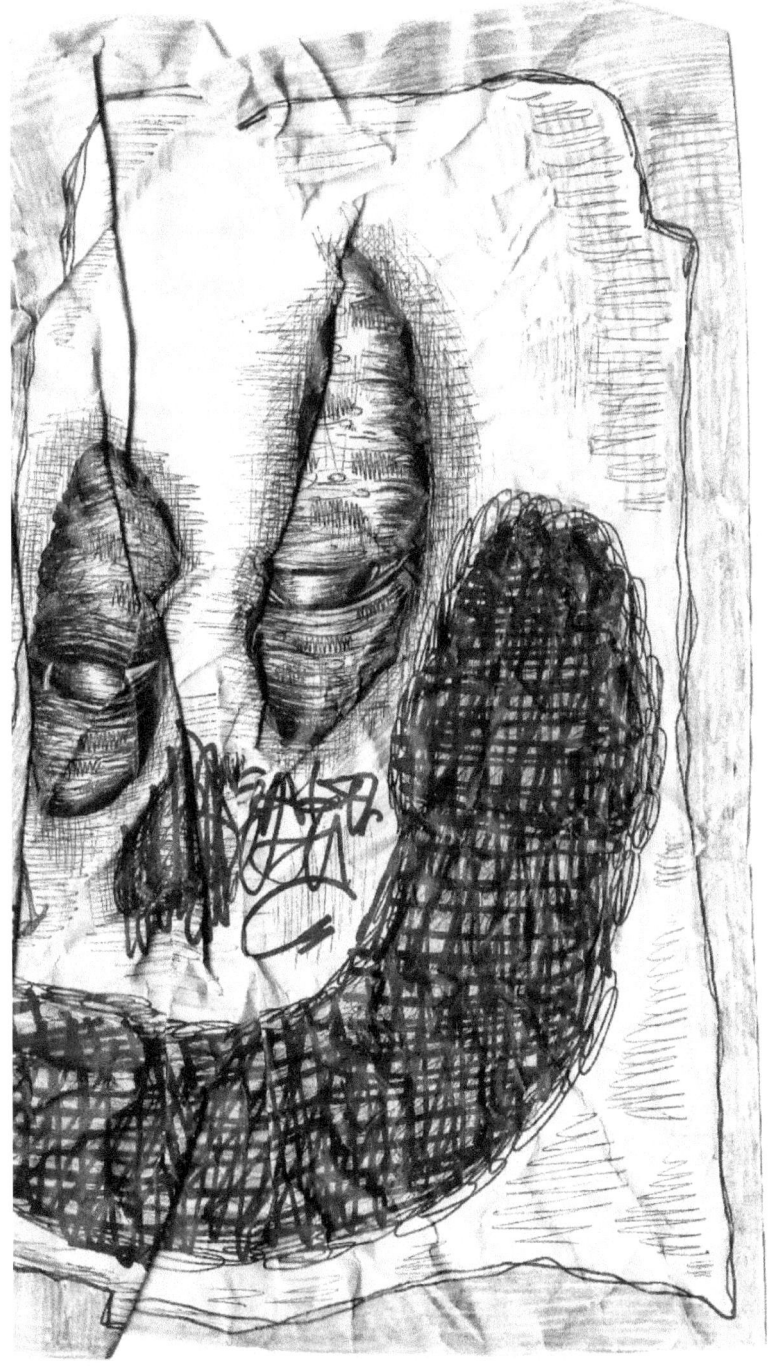

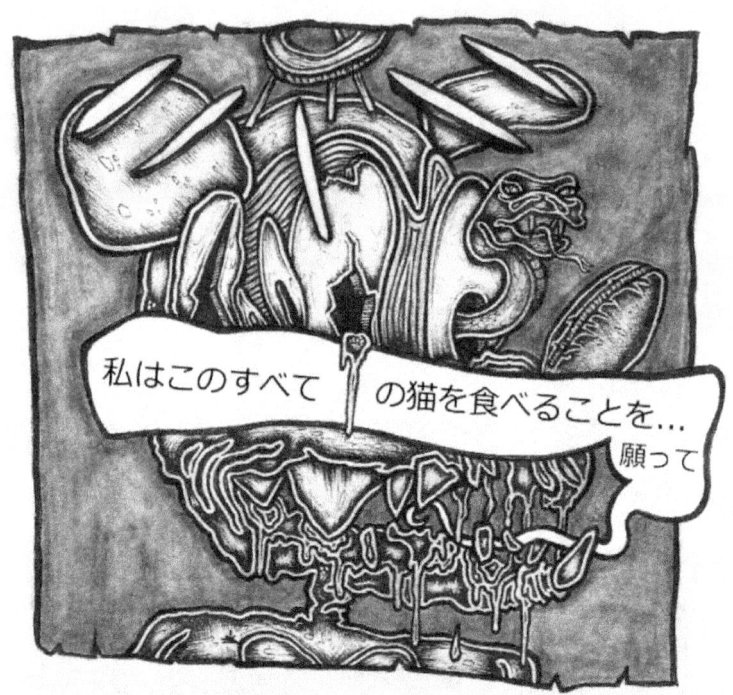

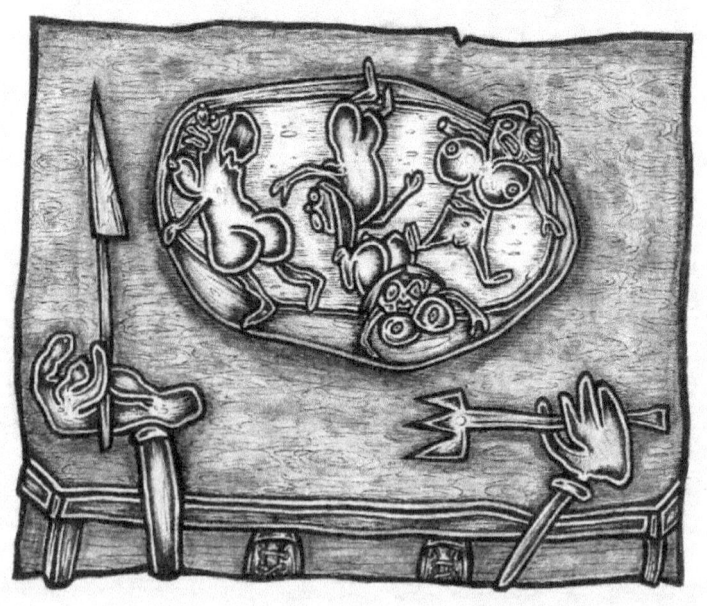

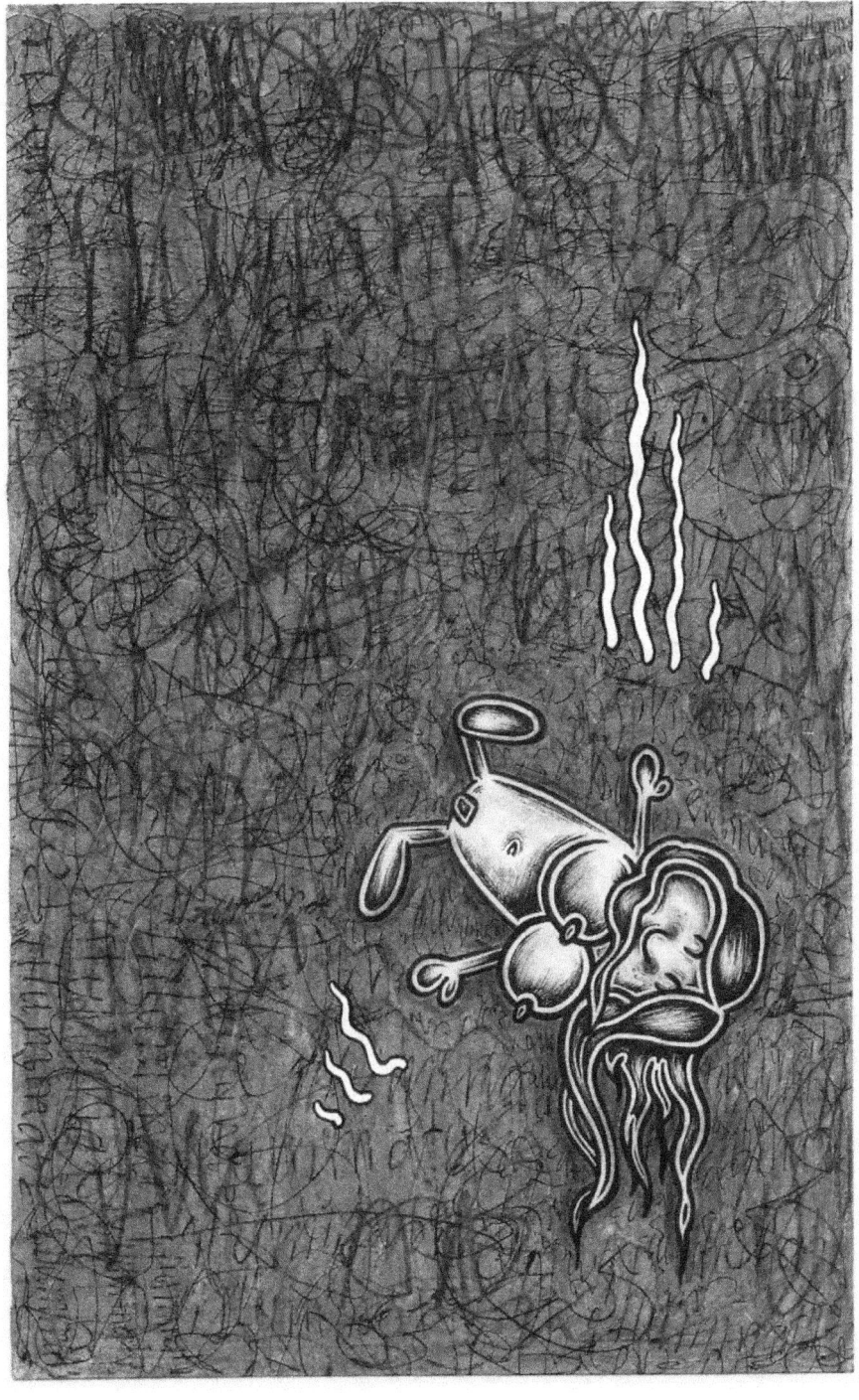

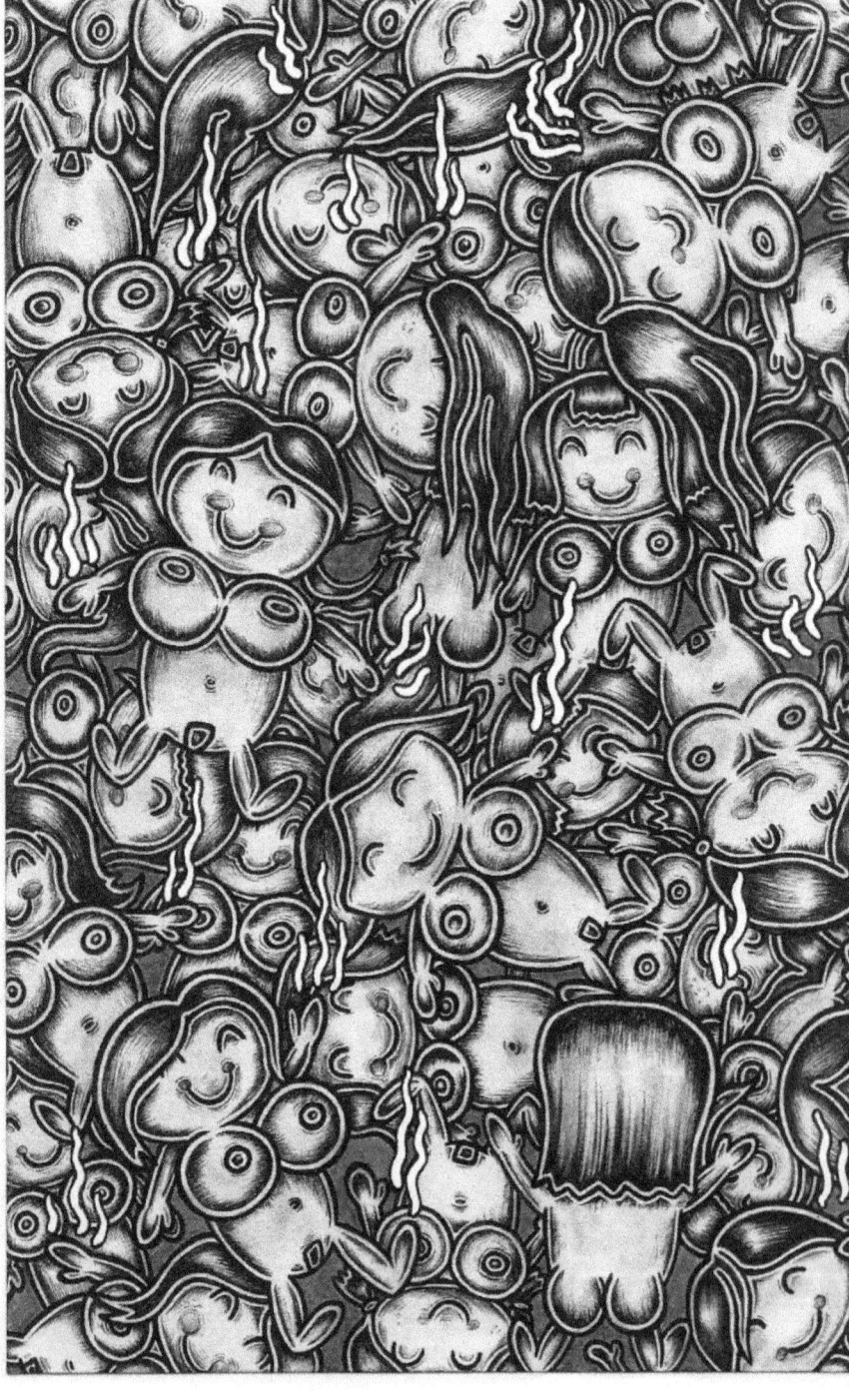

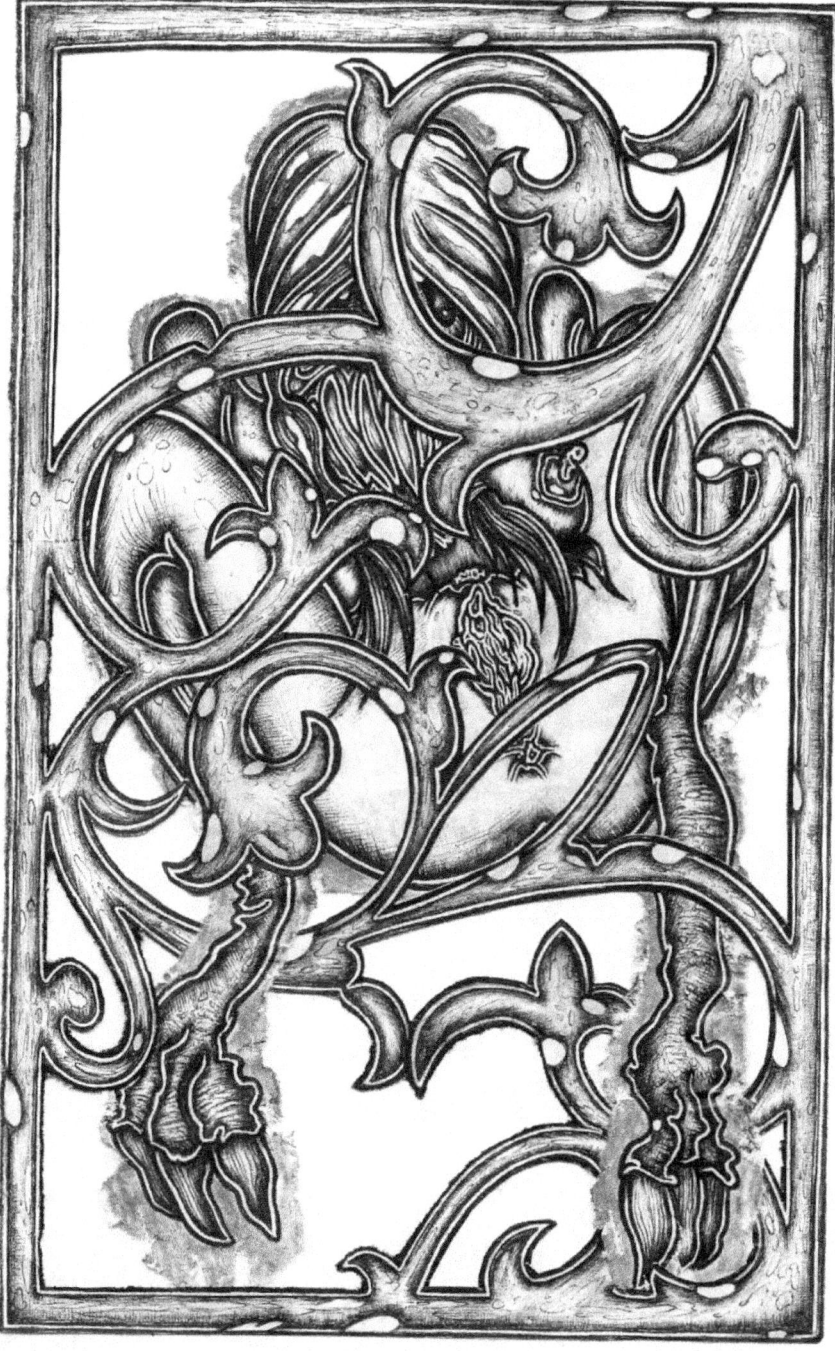

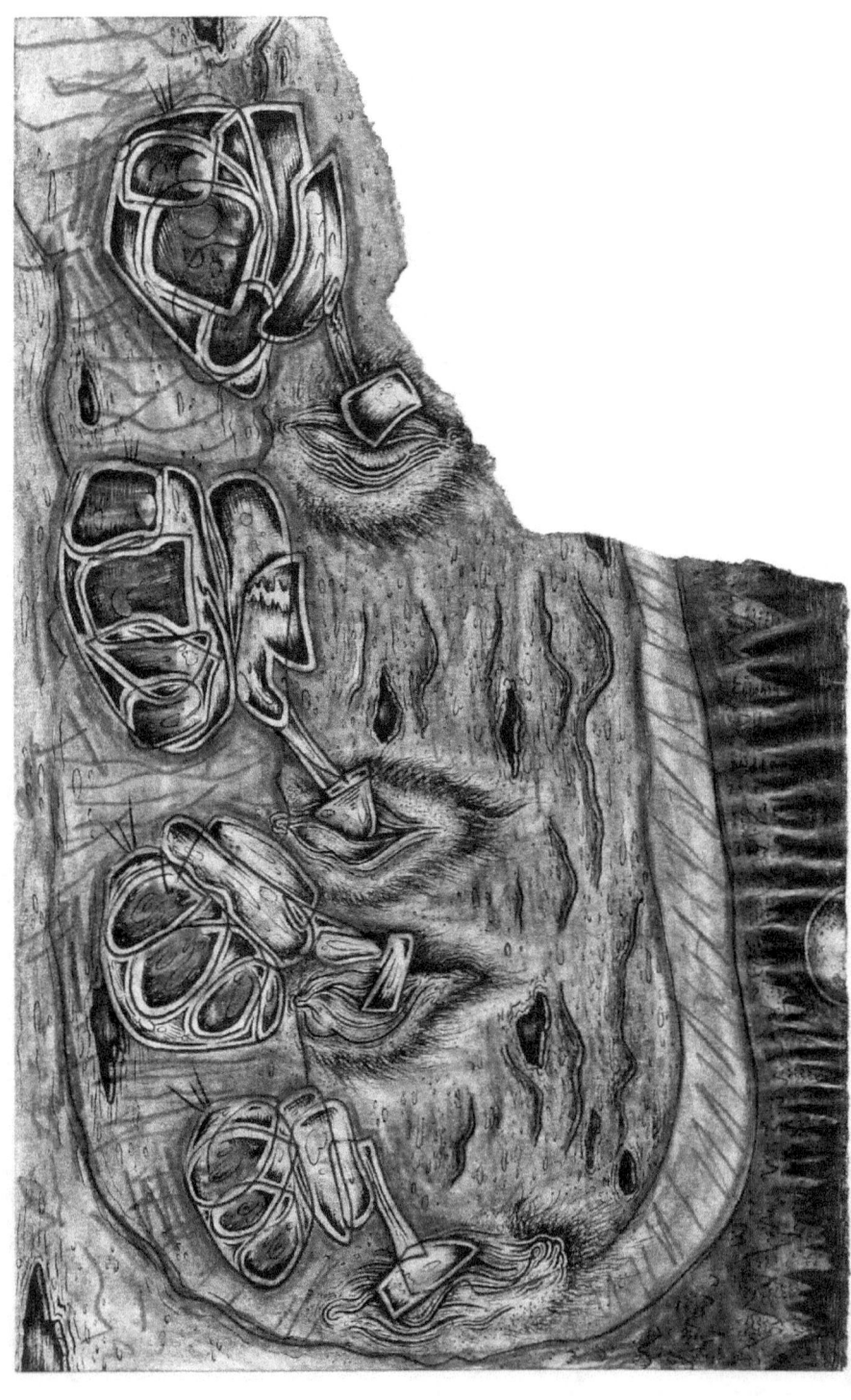

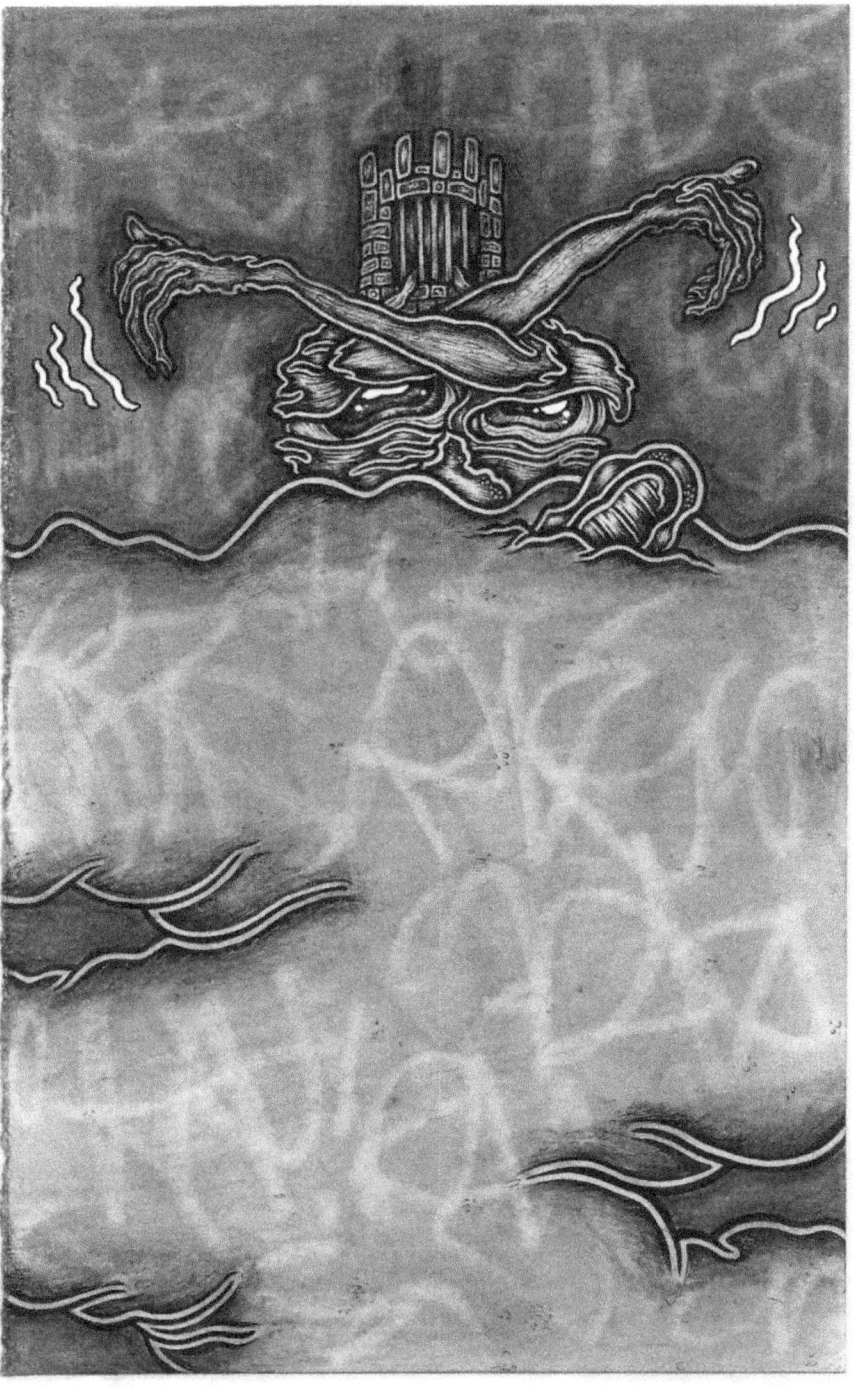

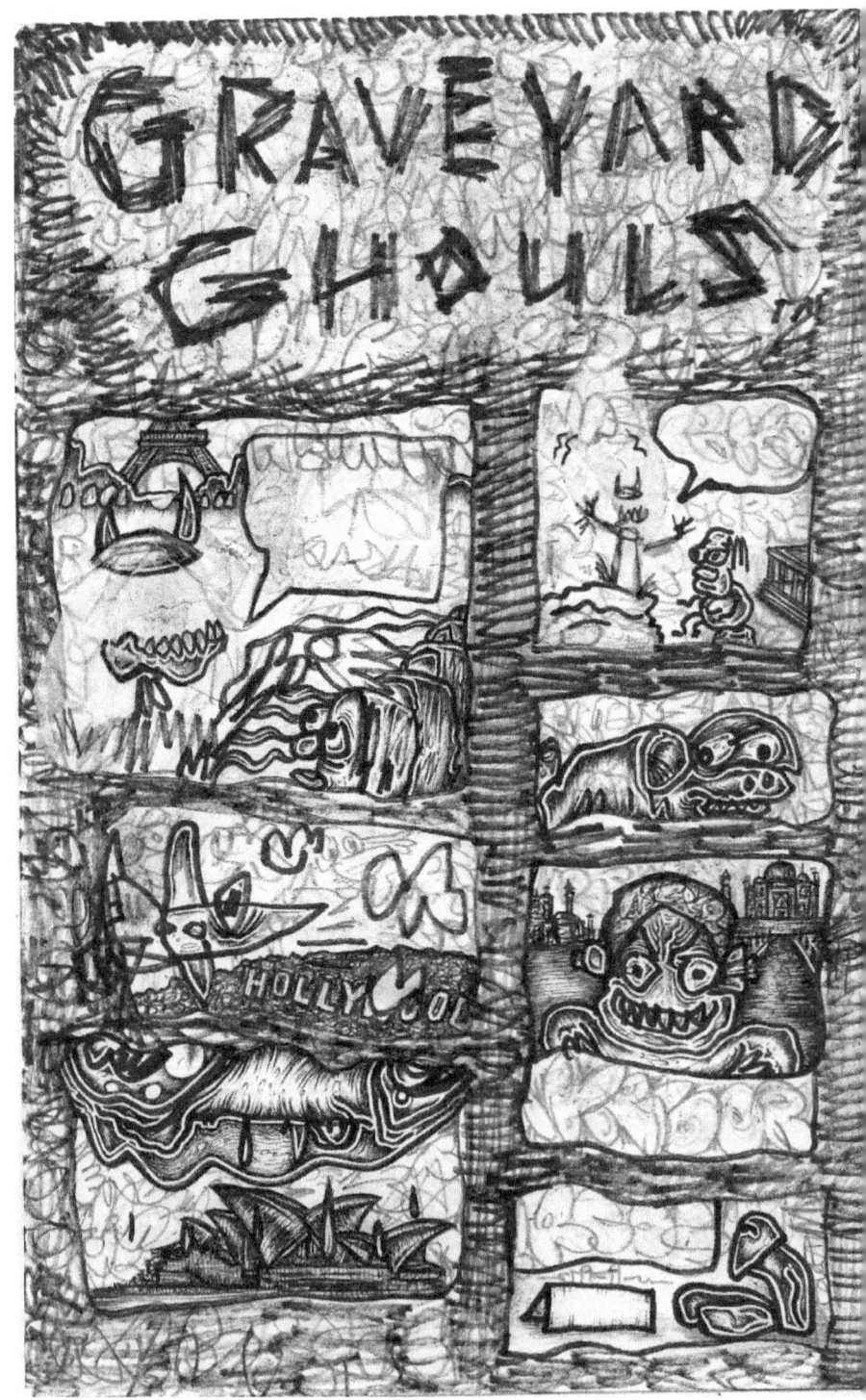

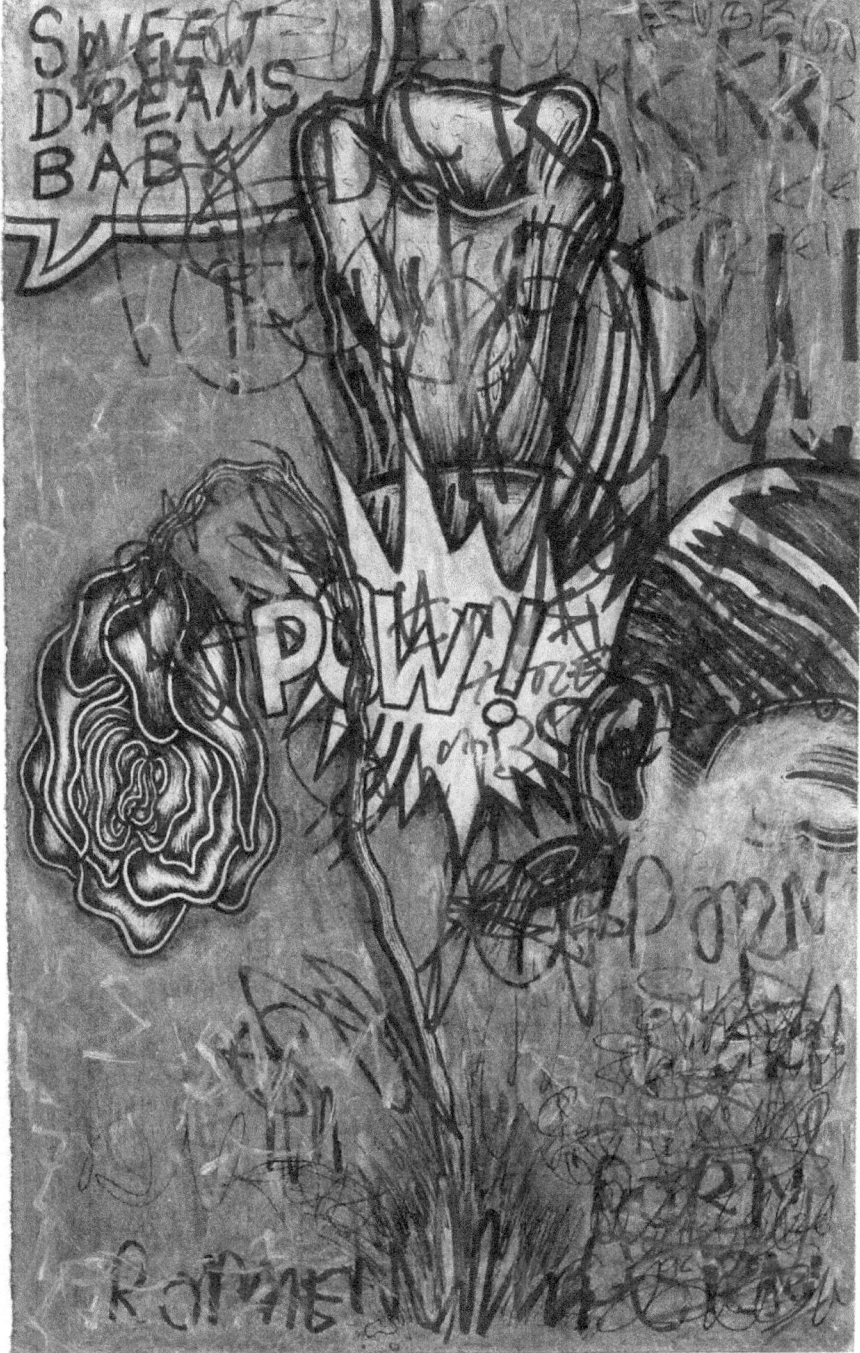

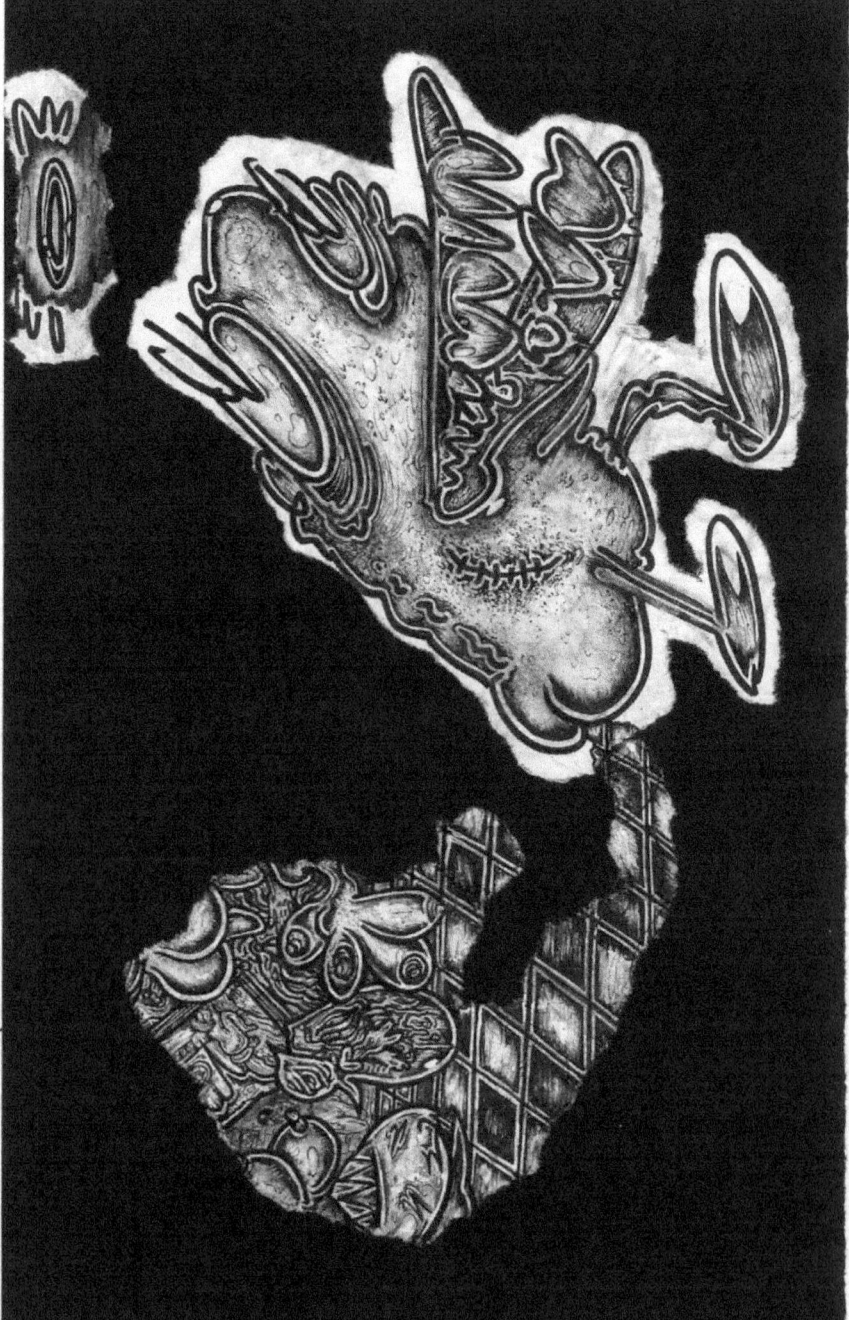

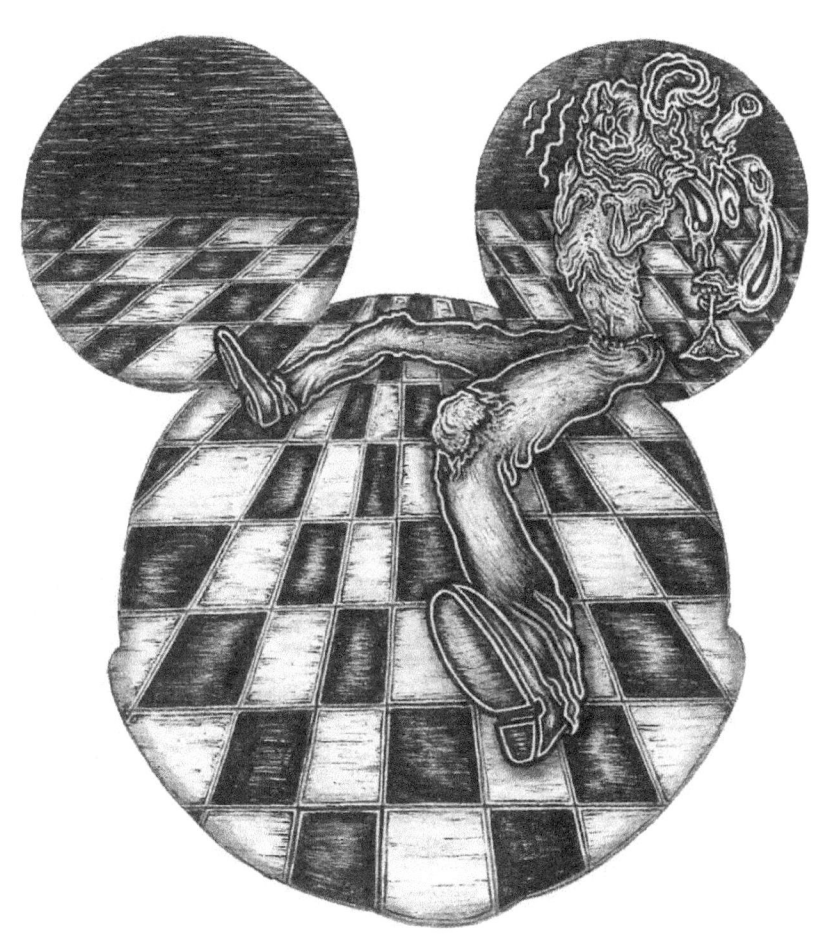

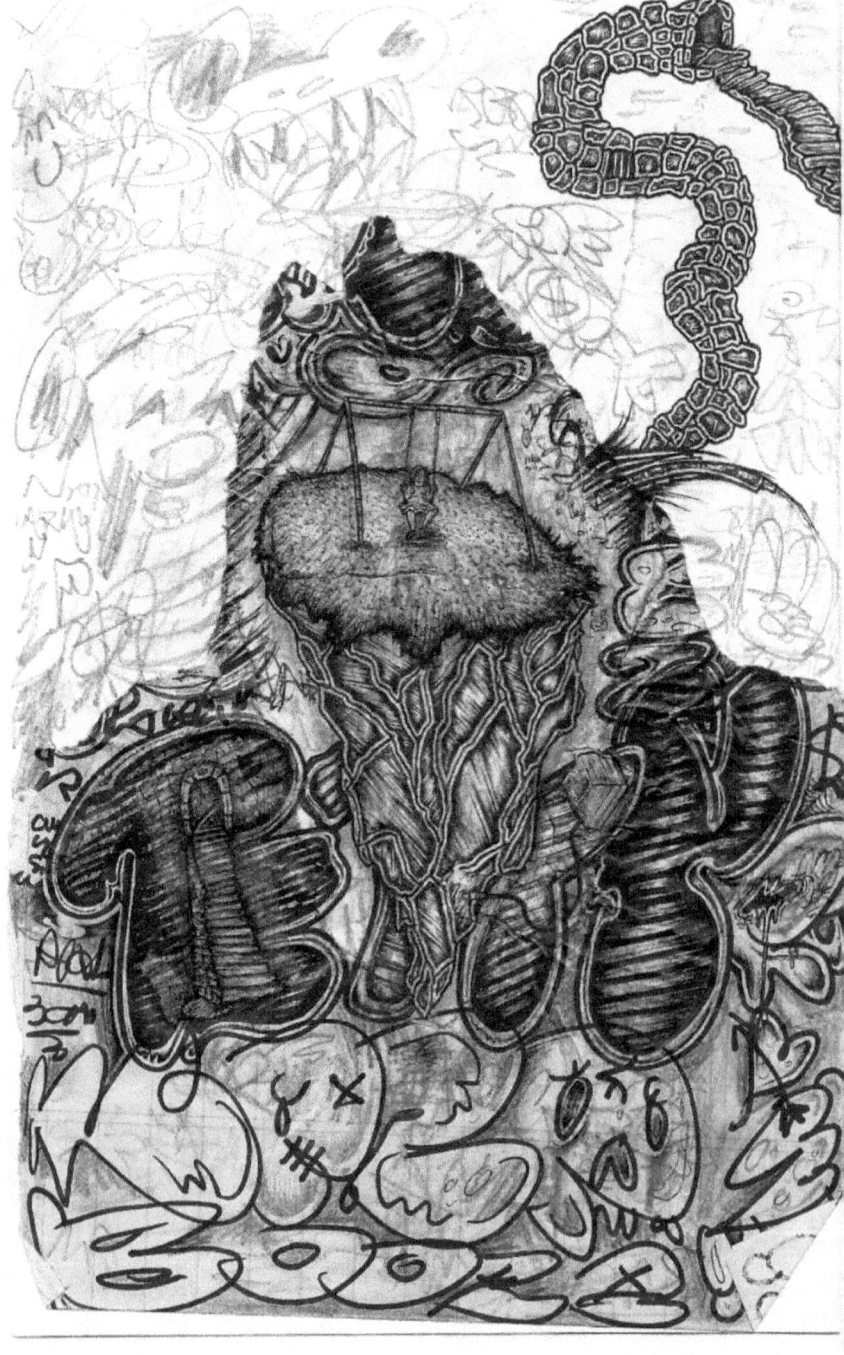

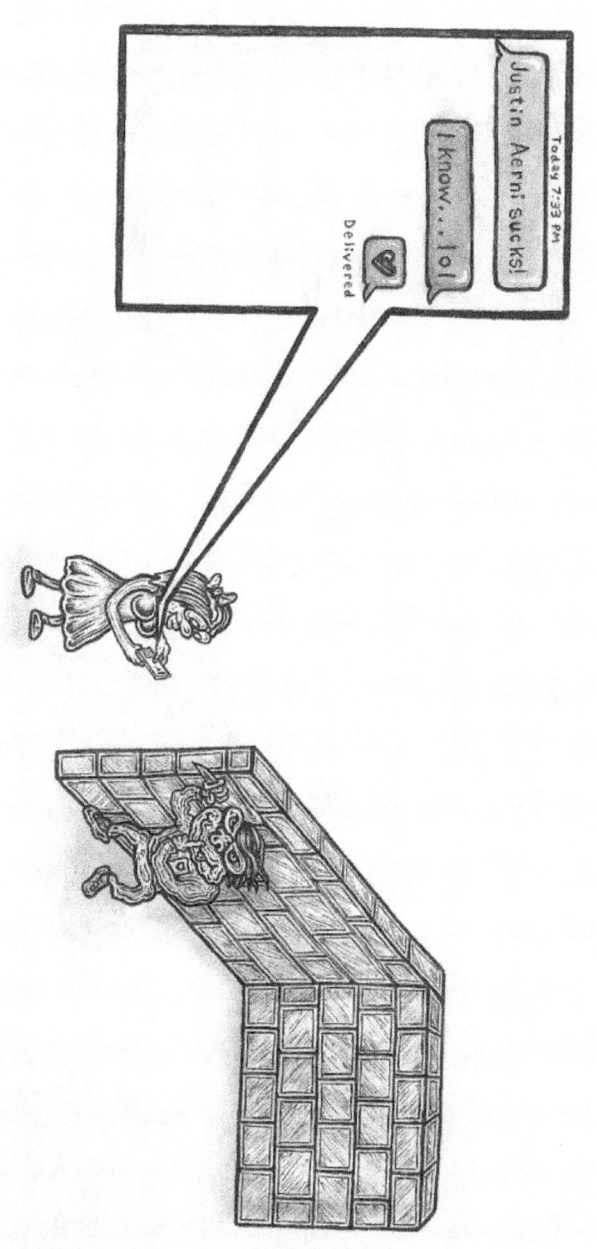

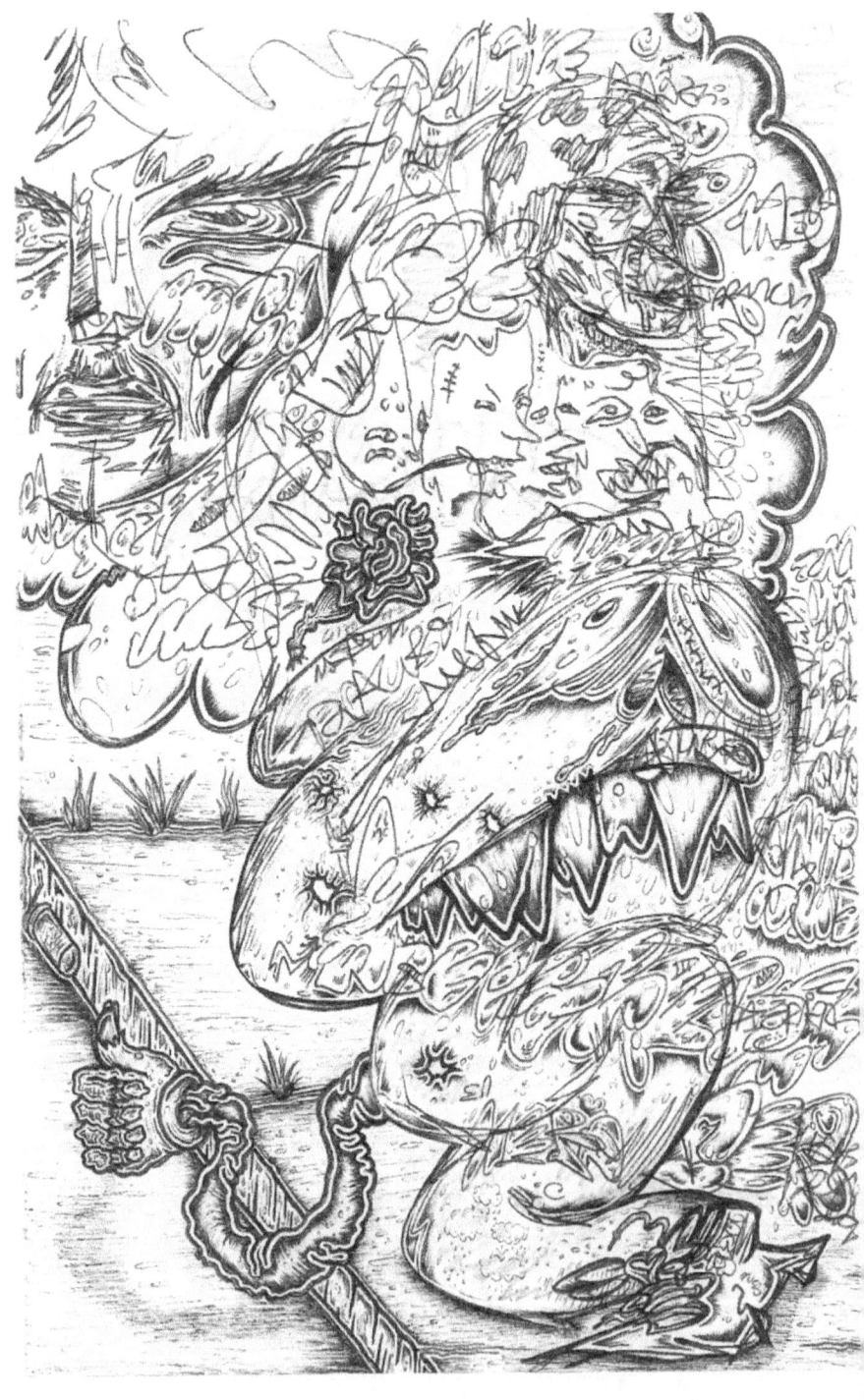

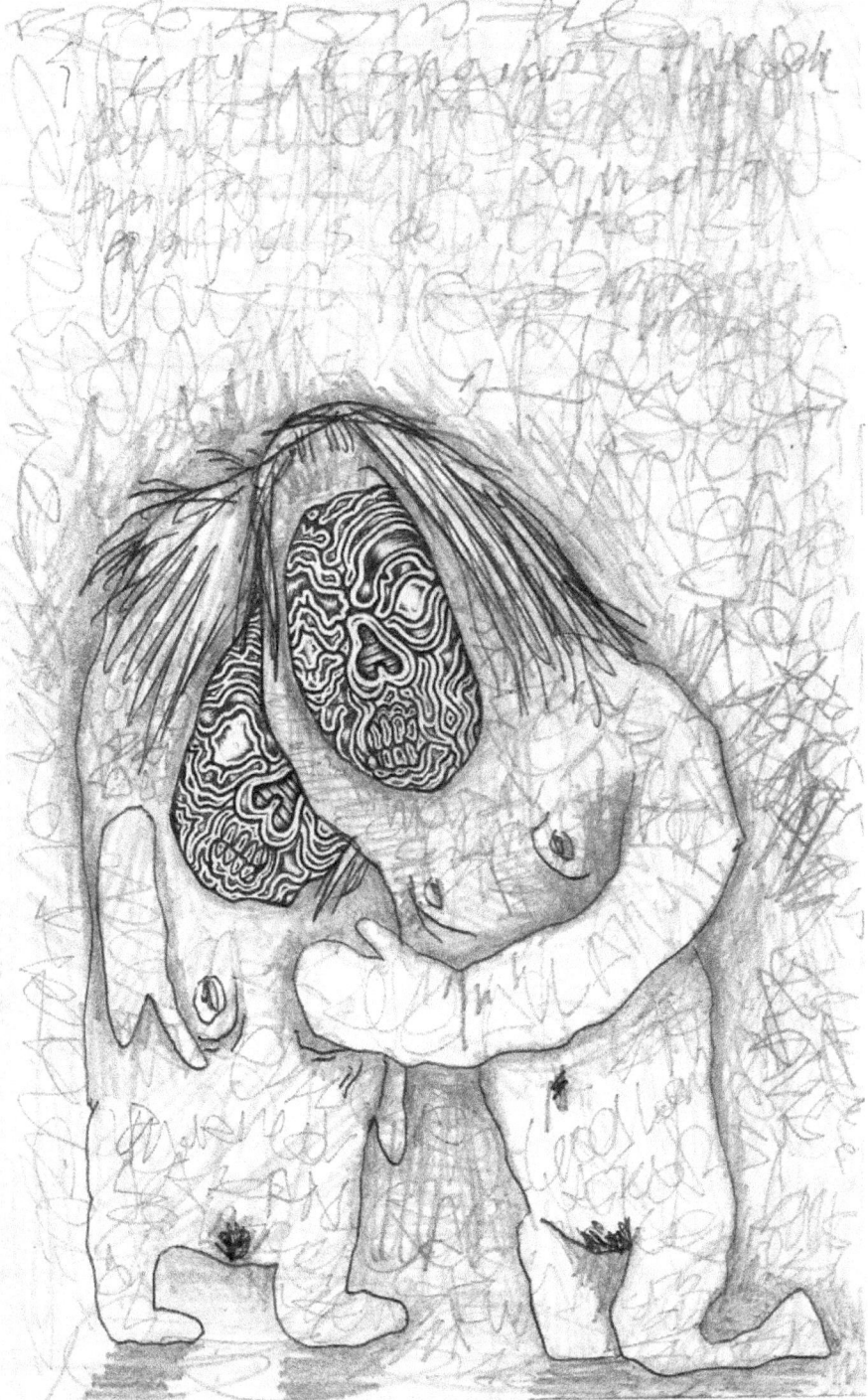

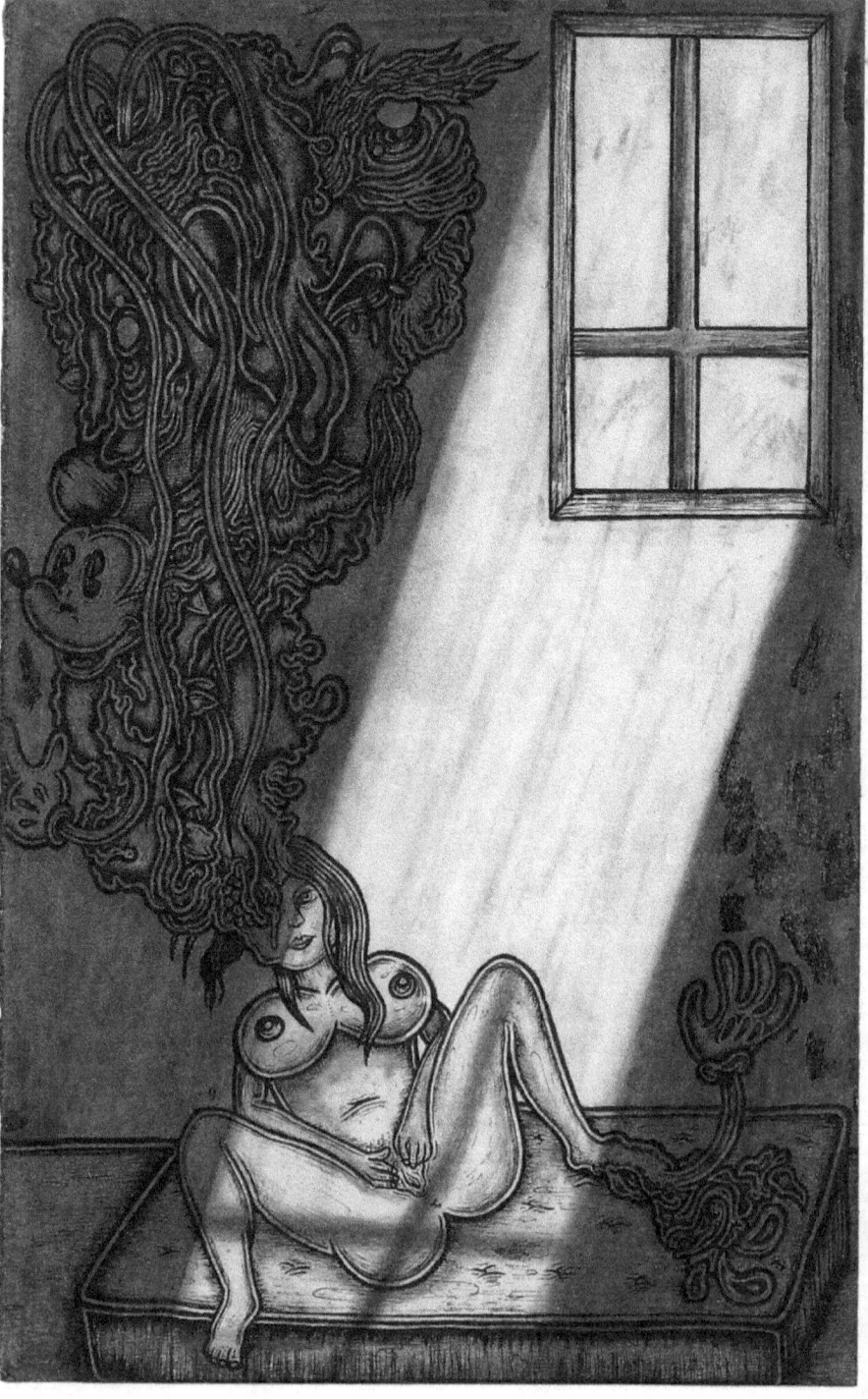

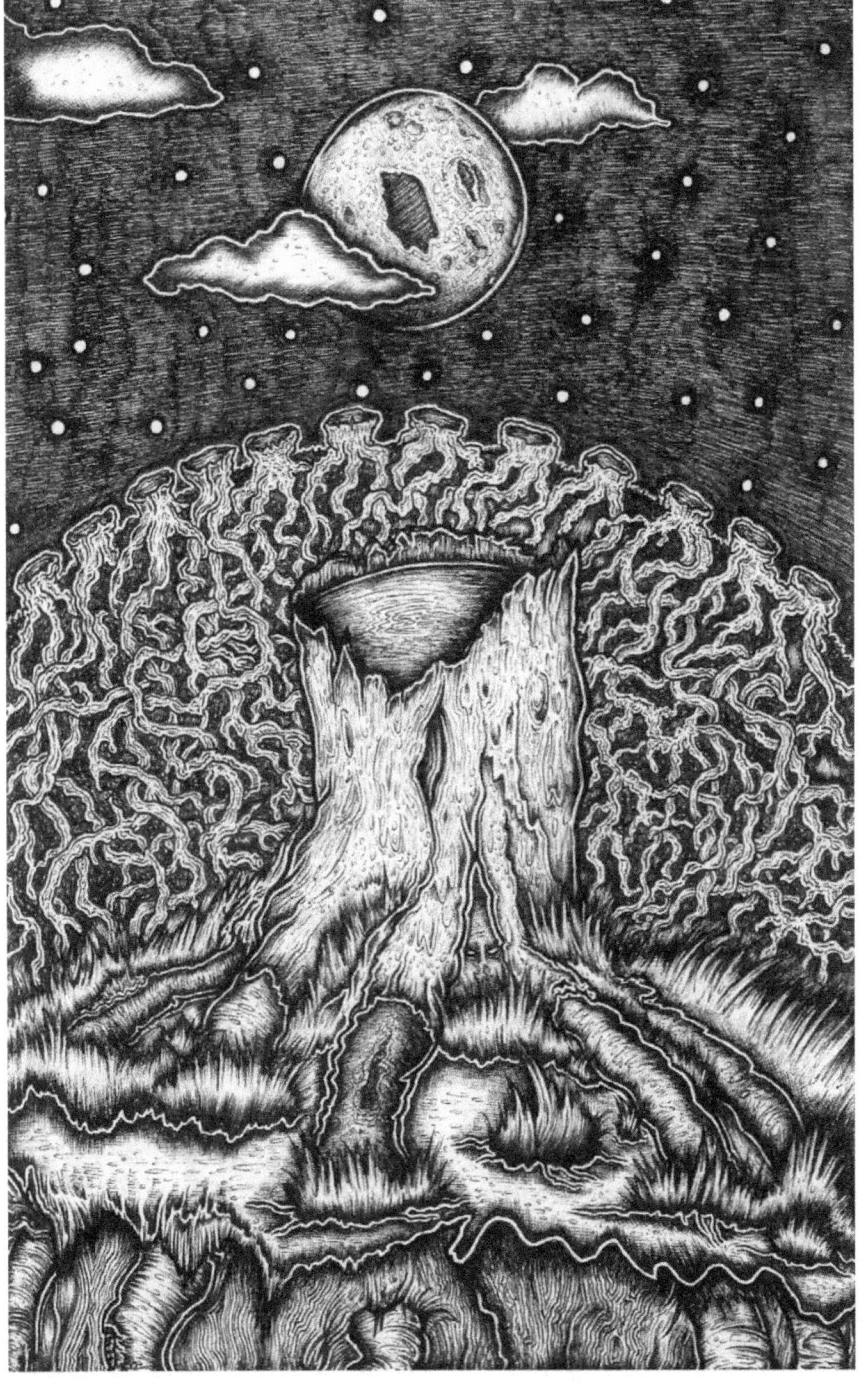

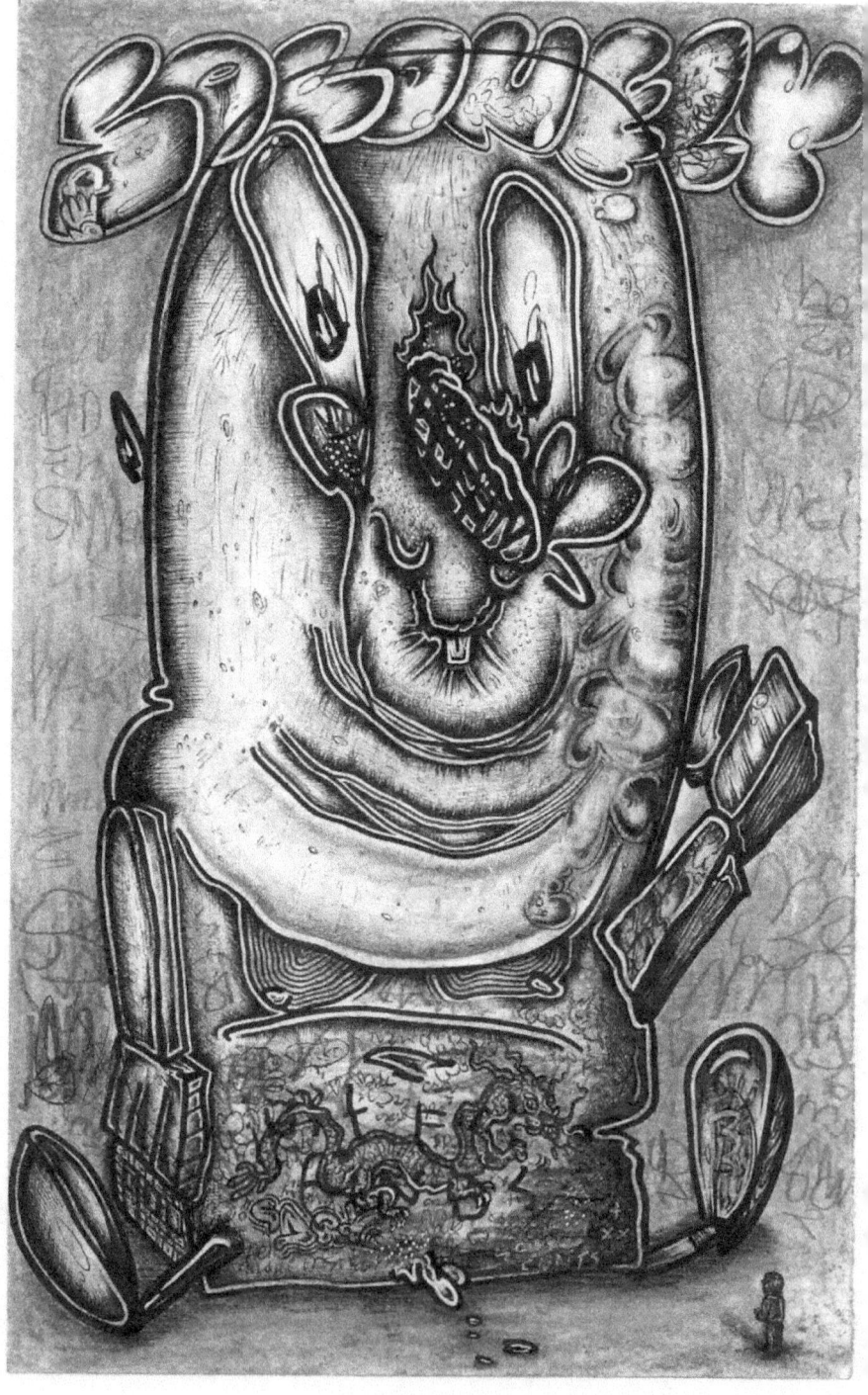

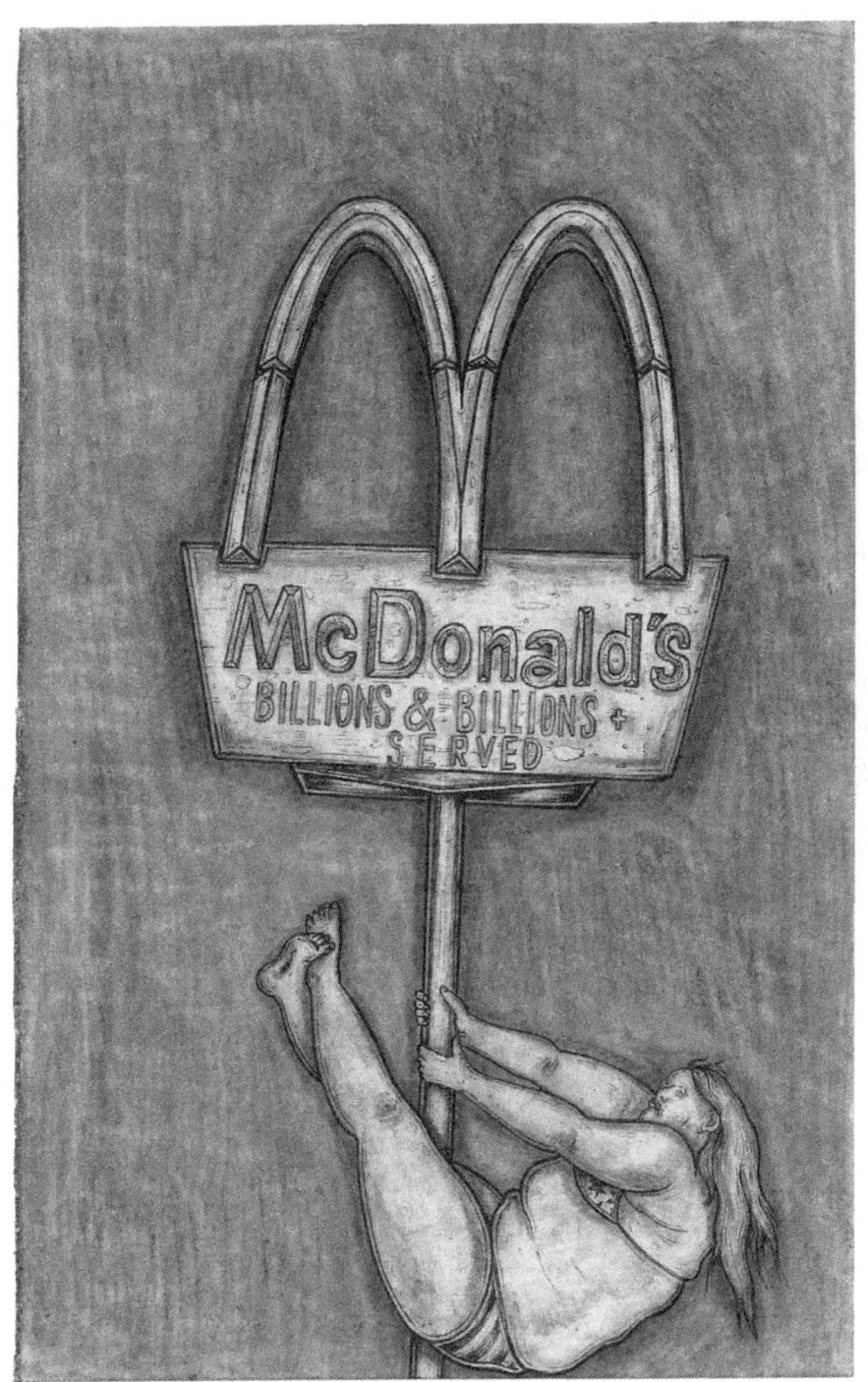

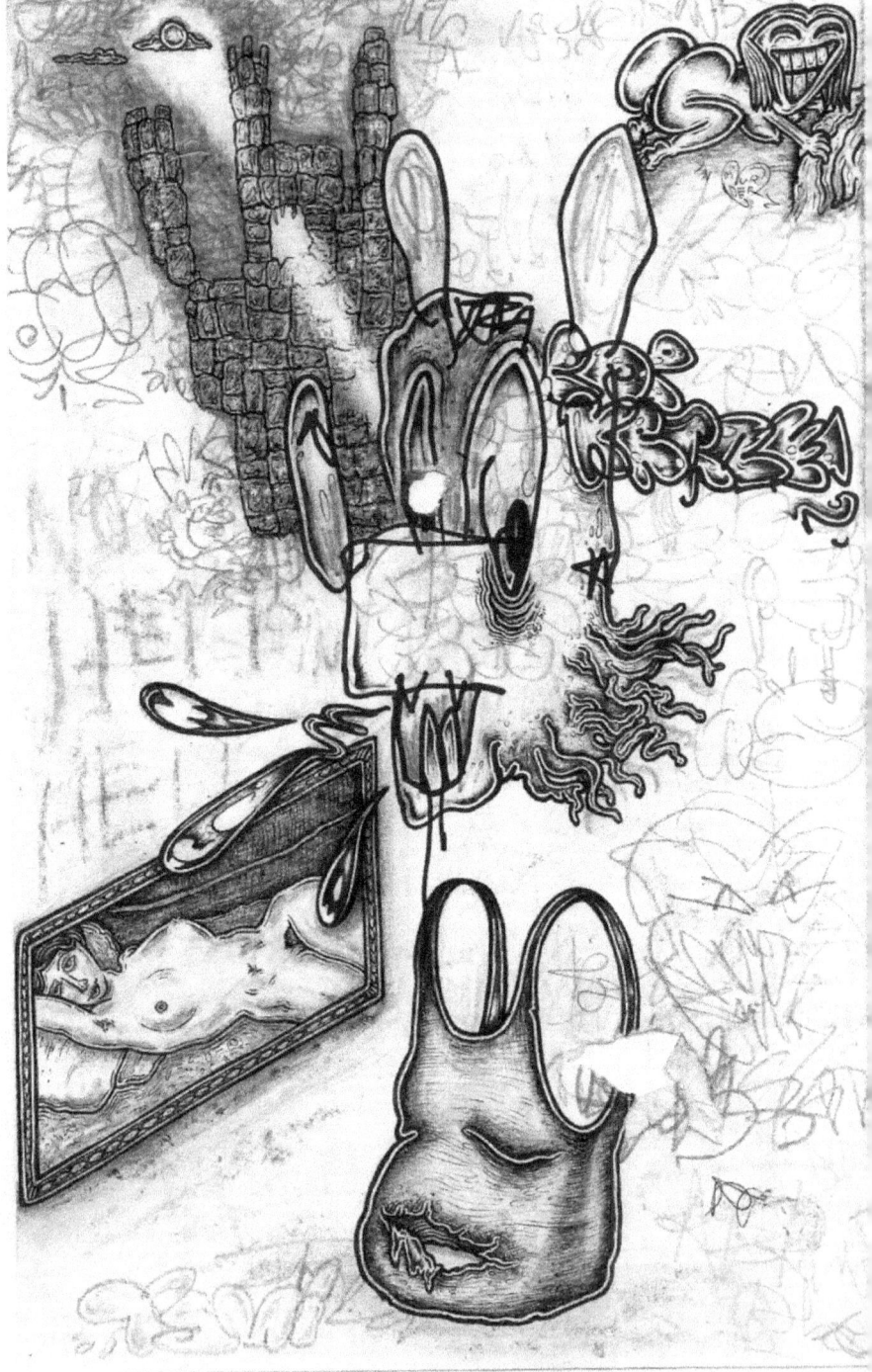

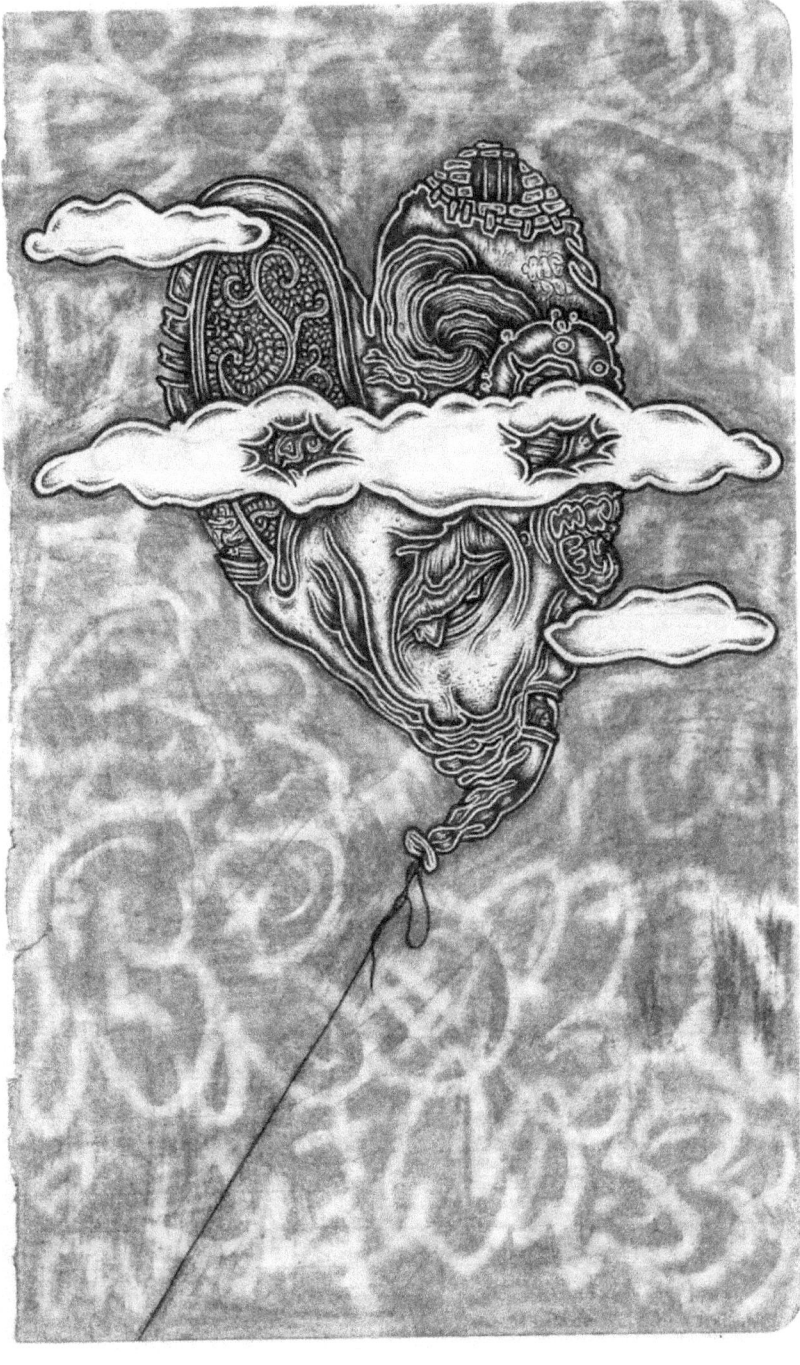

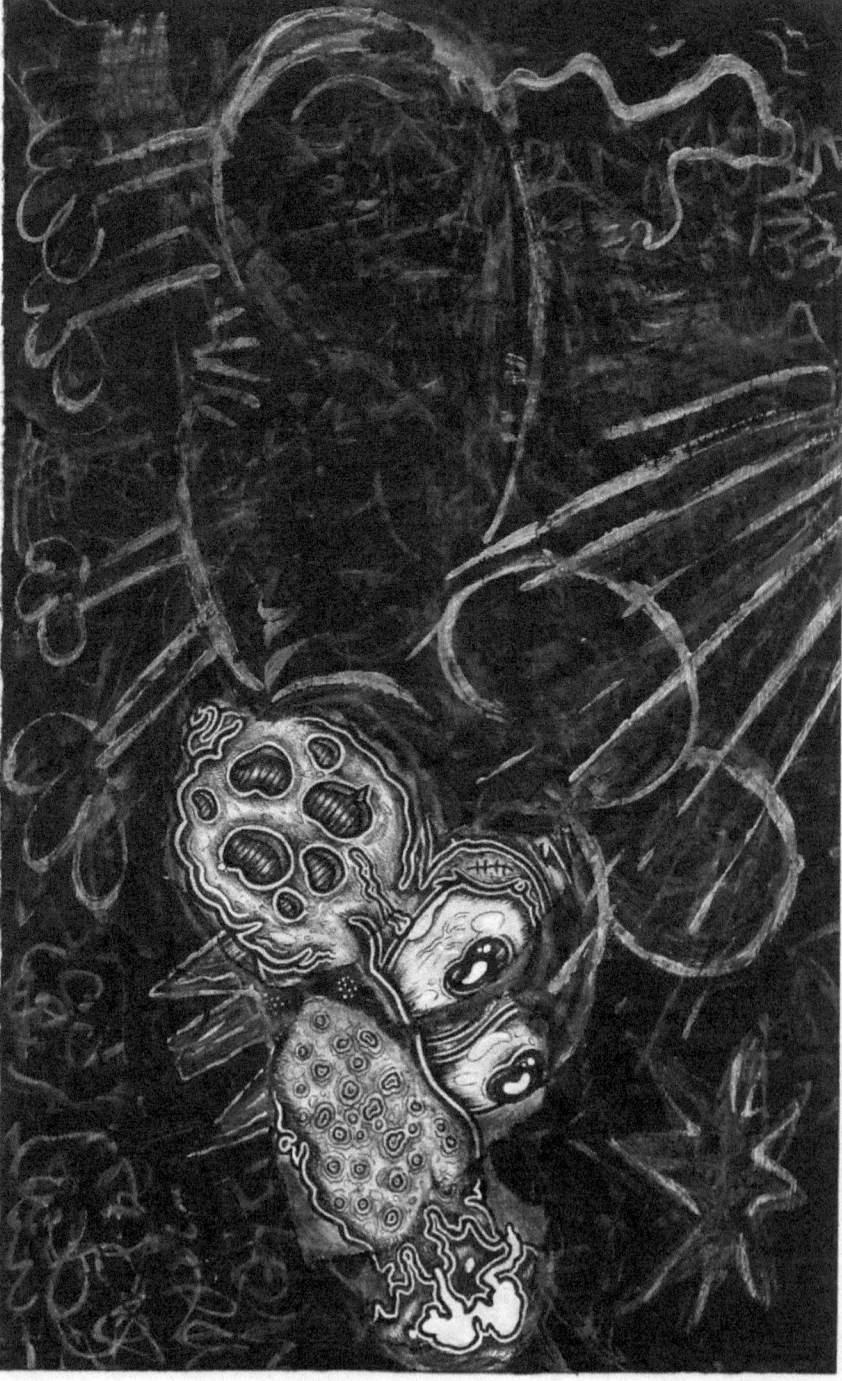

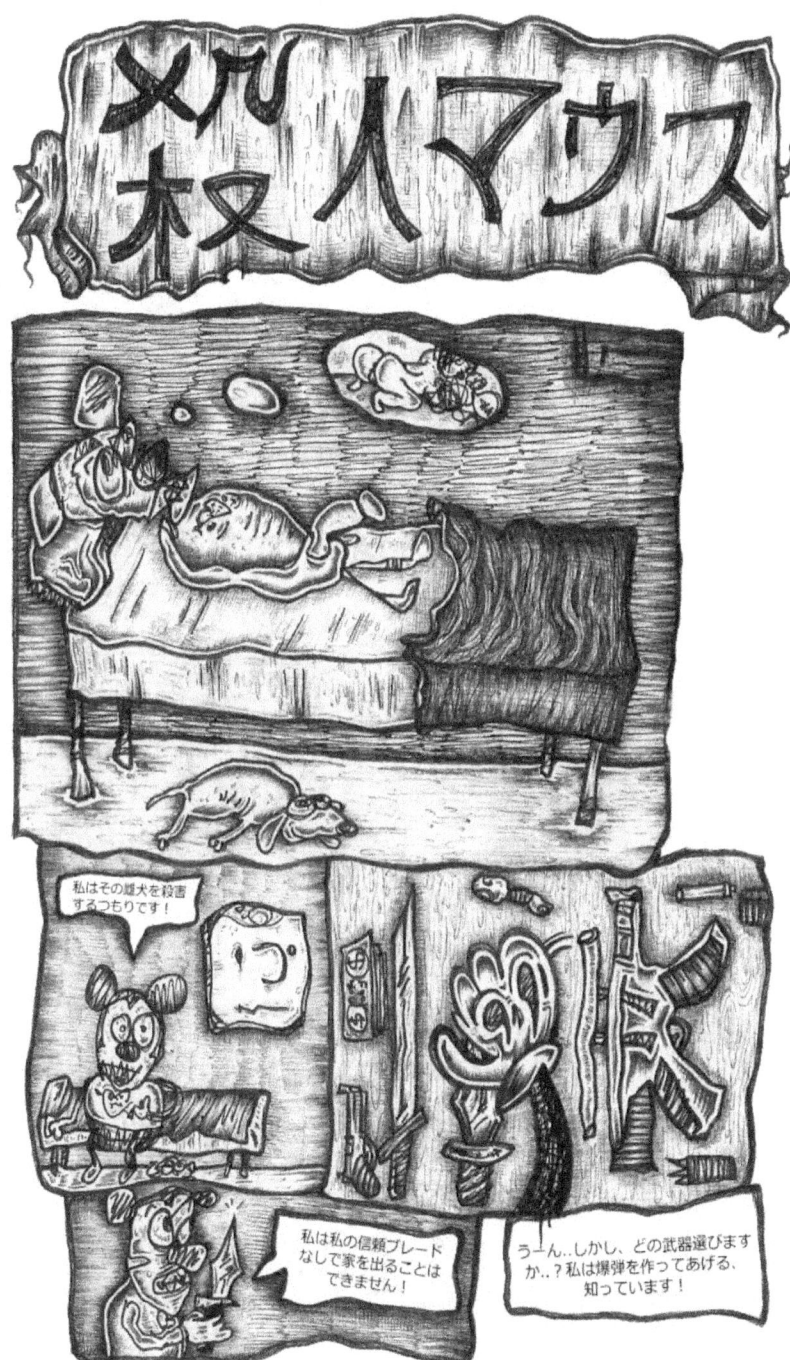

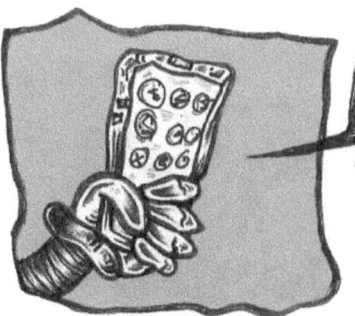

私が知っている、私は雌犬を呼び
出すだろうと私は、申し訳ありませ
んと思い、彼女を教えて...爆発！

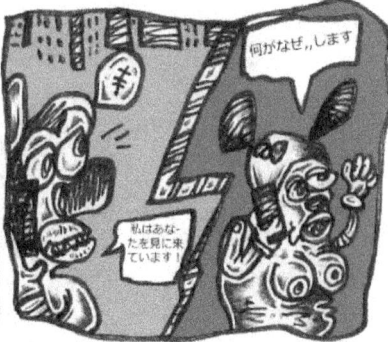

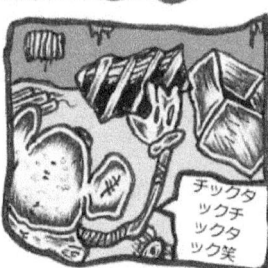

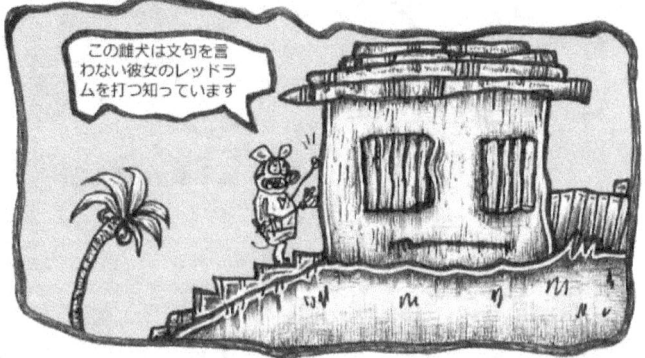

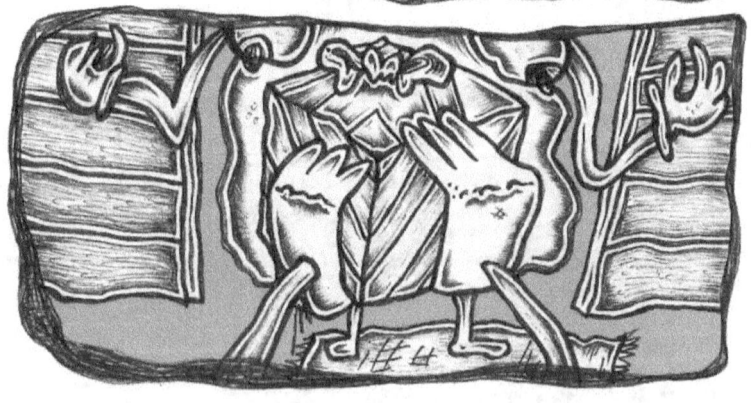

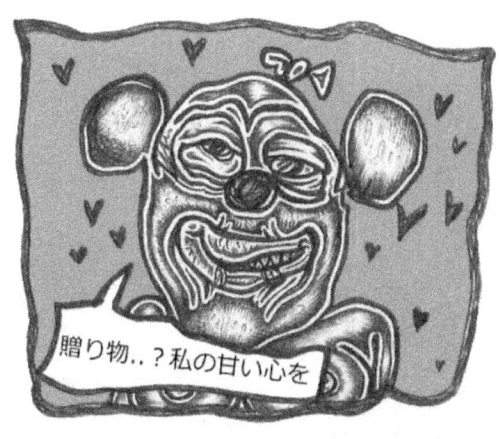

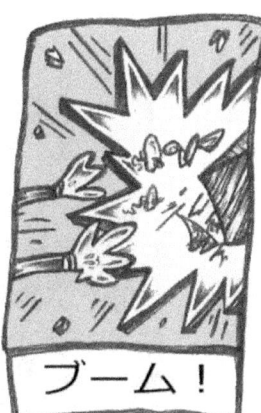

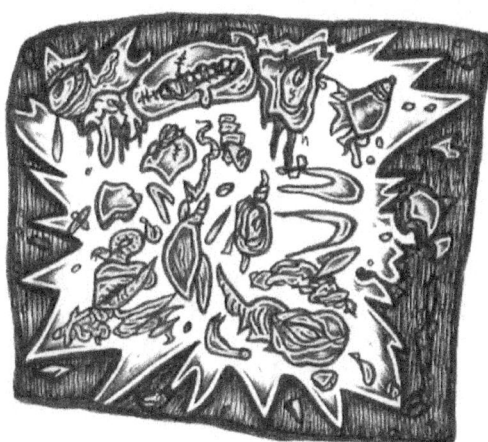

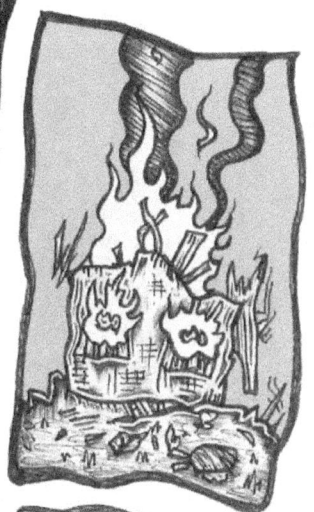

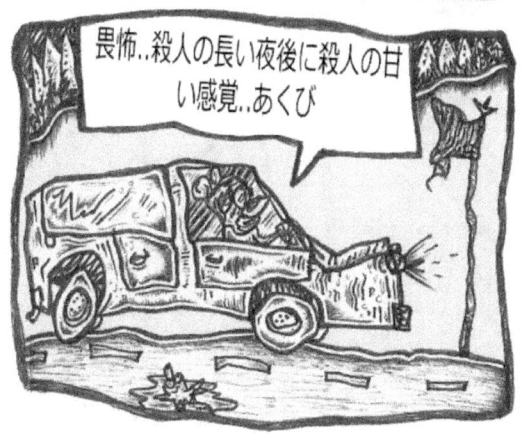

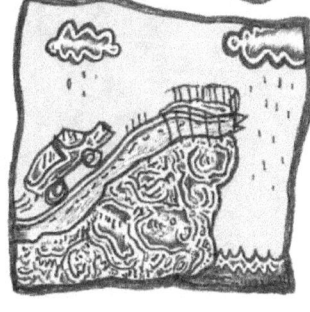

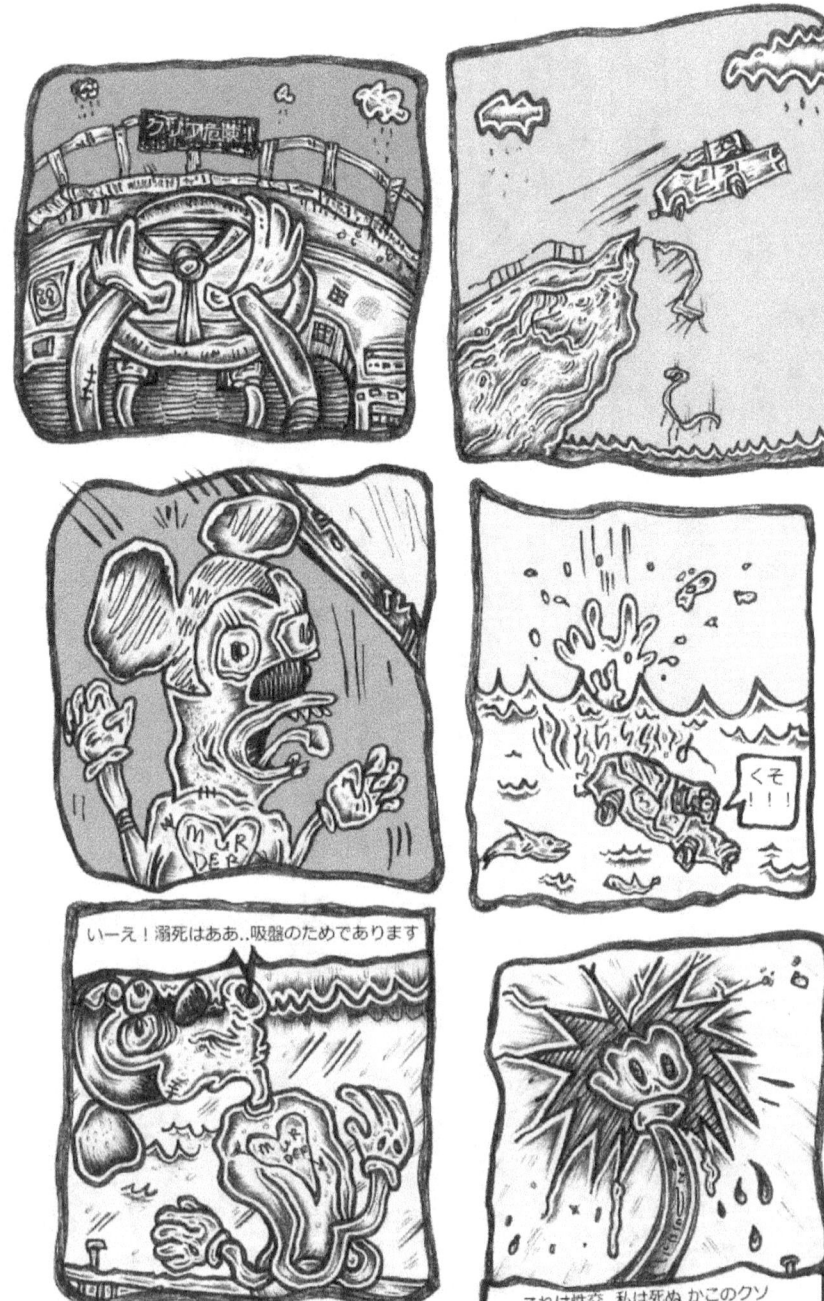

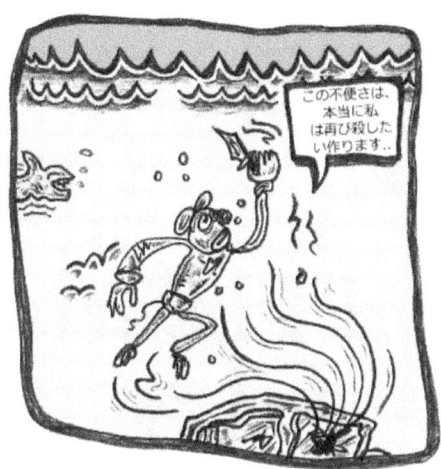

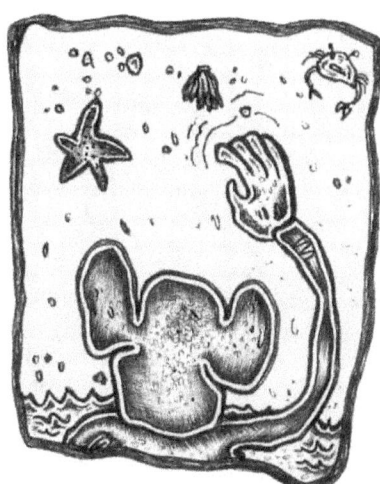

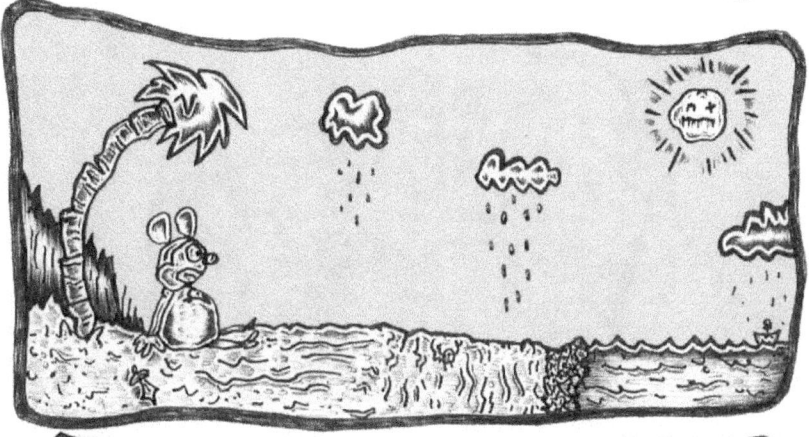

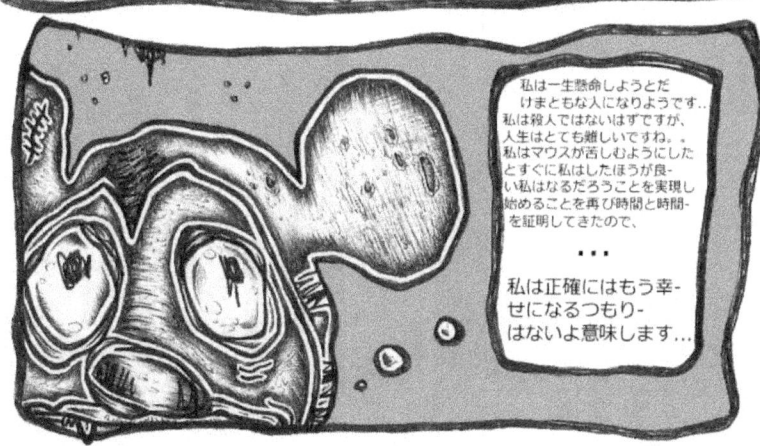

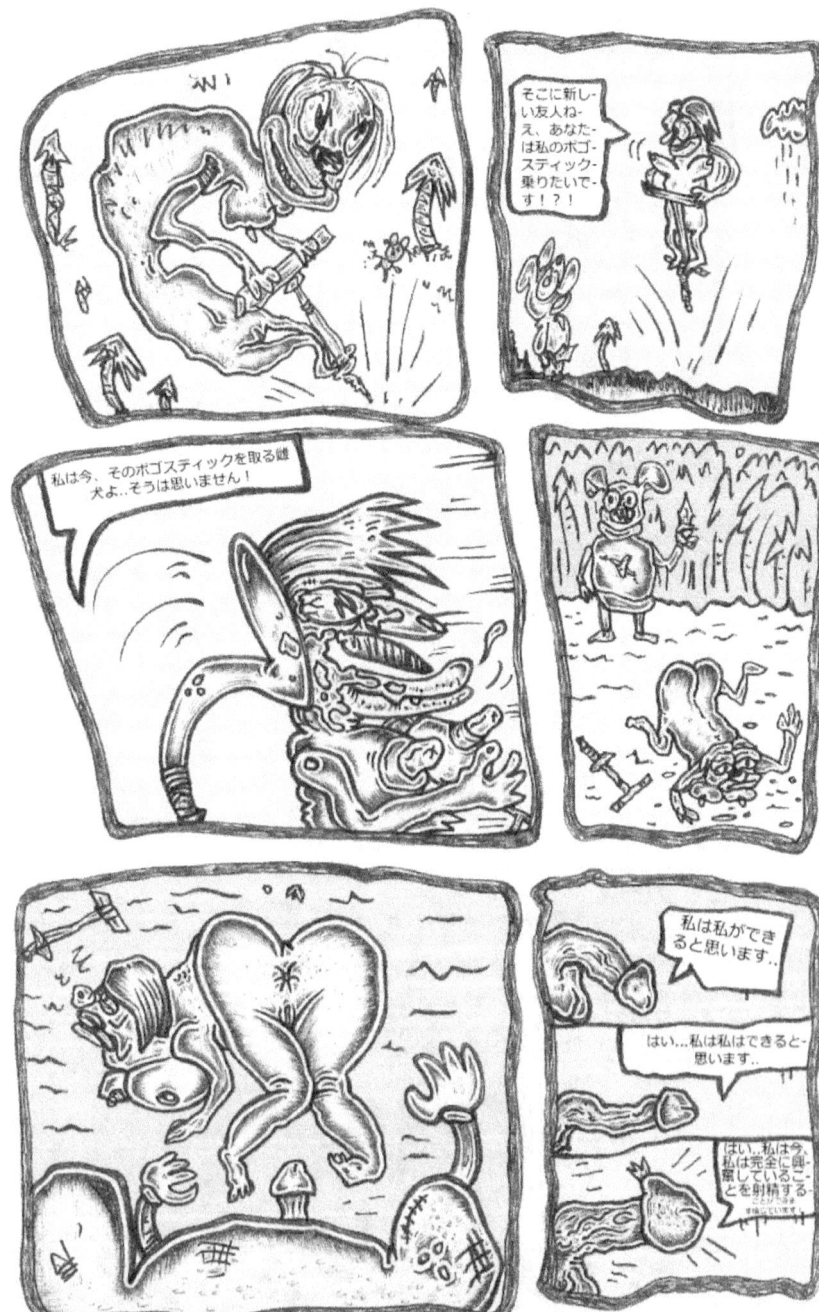

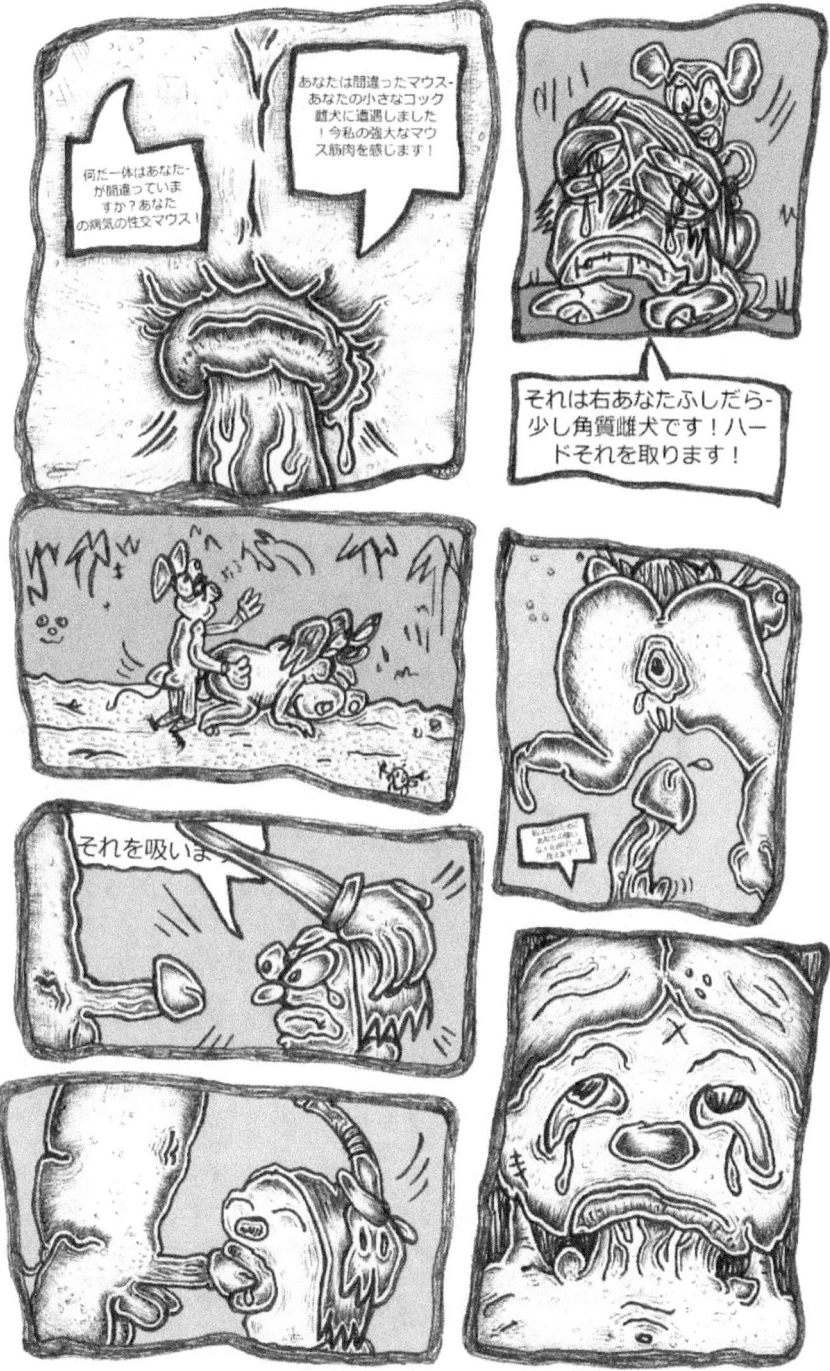

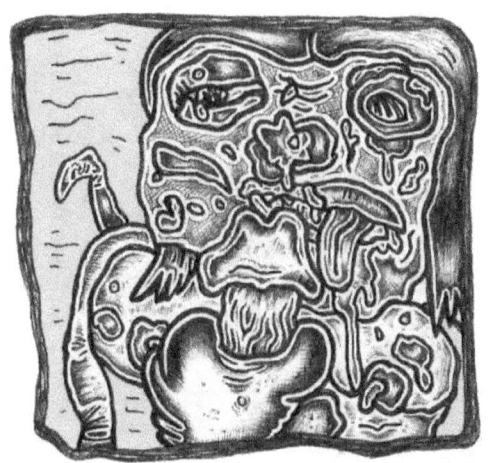

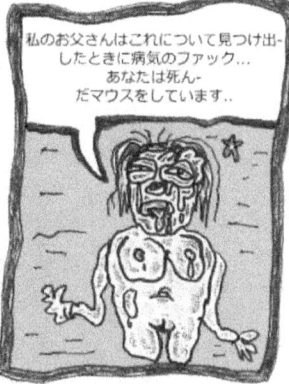

私のお父さんはこれについて見つけ出し
たときに病気のファック...
あなたは死ん-
だマウスをしています..

いいえいいえ..
あなたは何クソアイ-
デア誰が雌犬-
とあなたのクソを持-
っていません！
殺人のための時間！

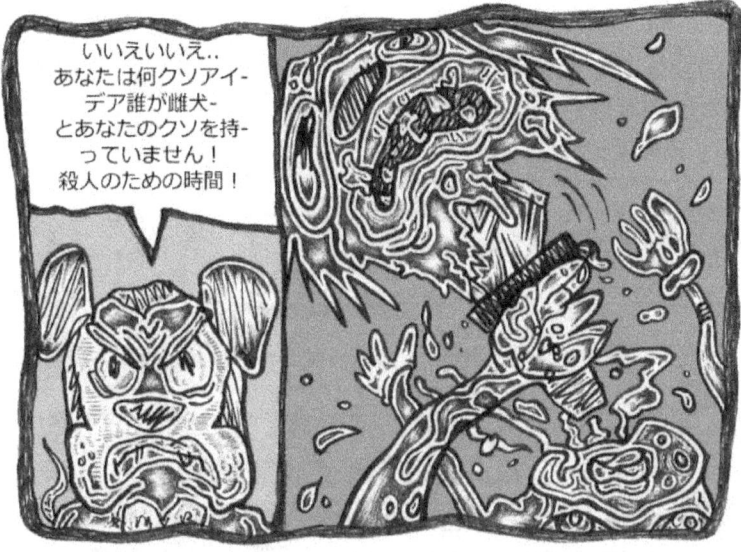

このポゴスティックは、今感じるんどのように少し雌犬！笑。
伝説の殺人マウスと性交することはありません！

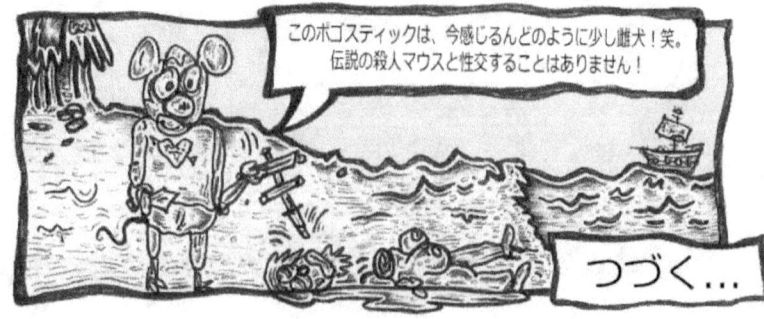

つづく...

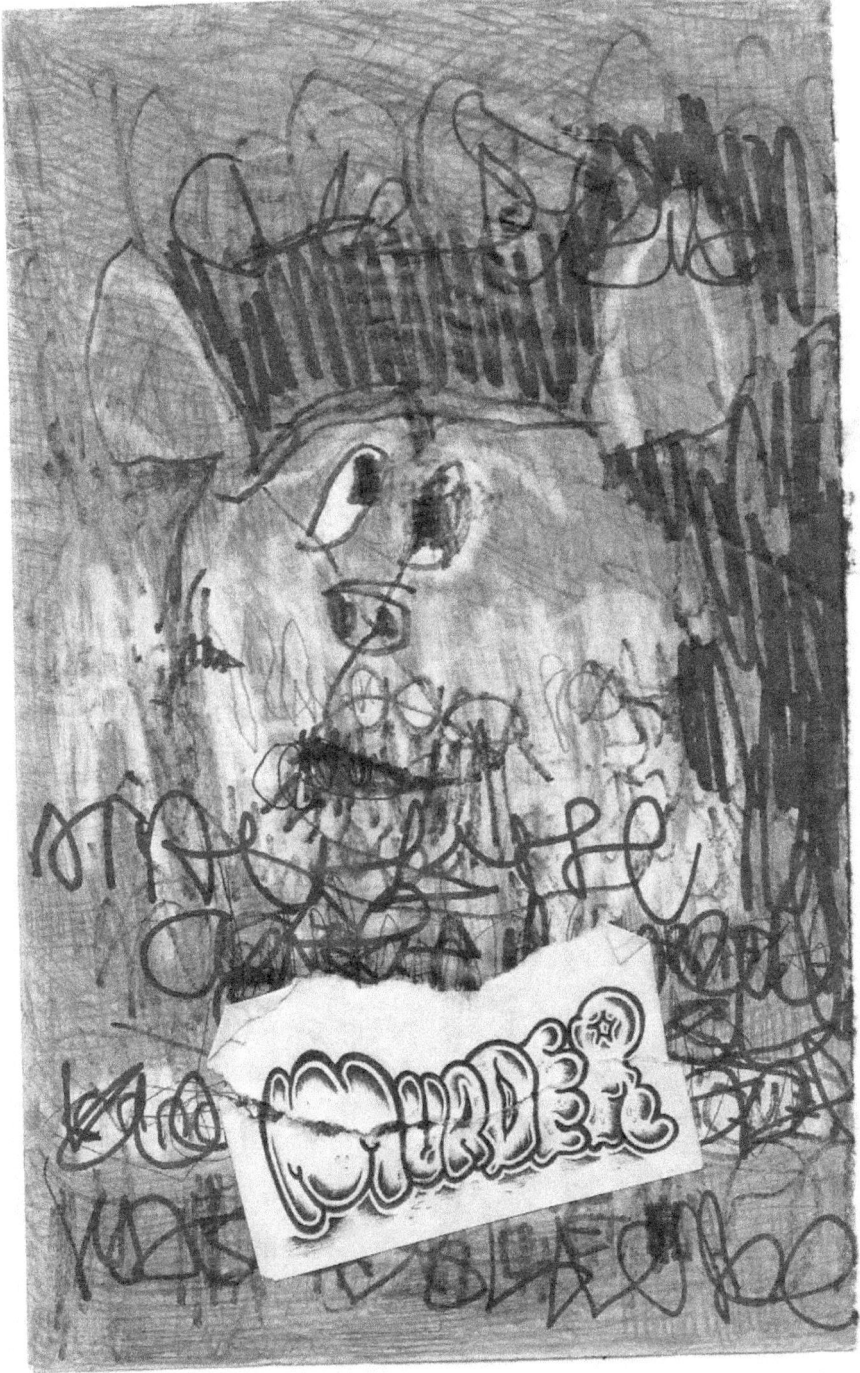

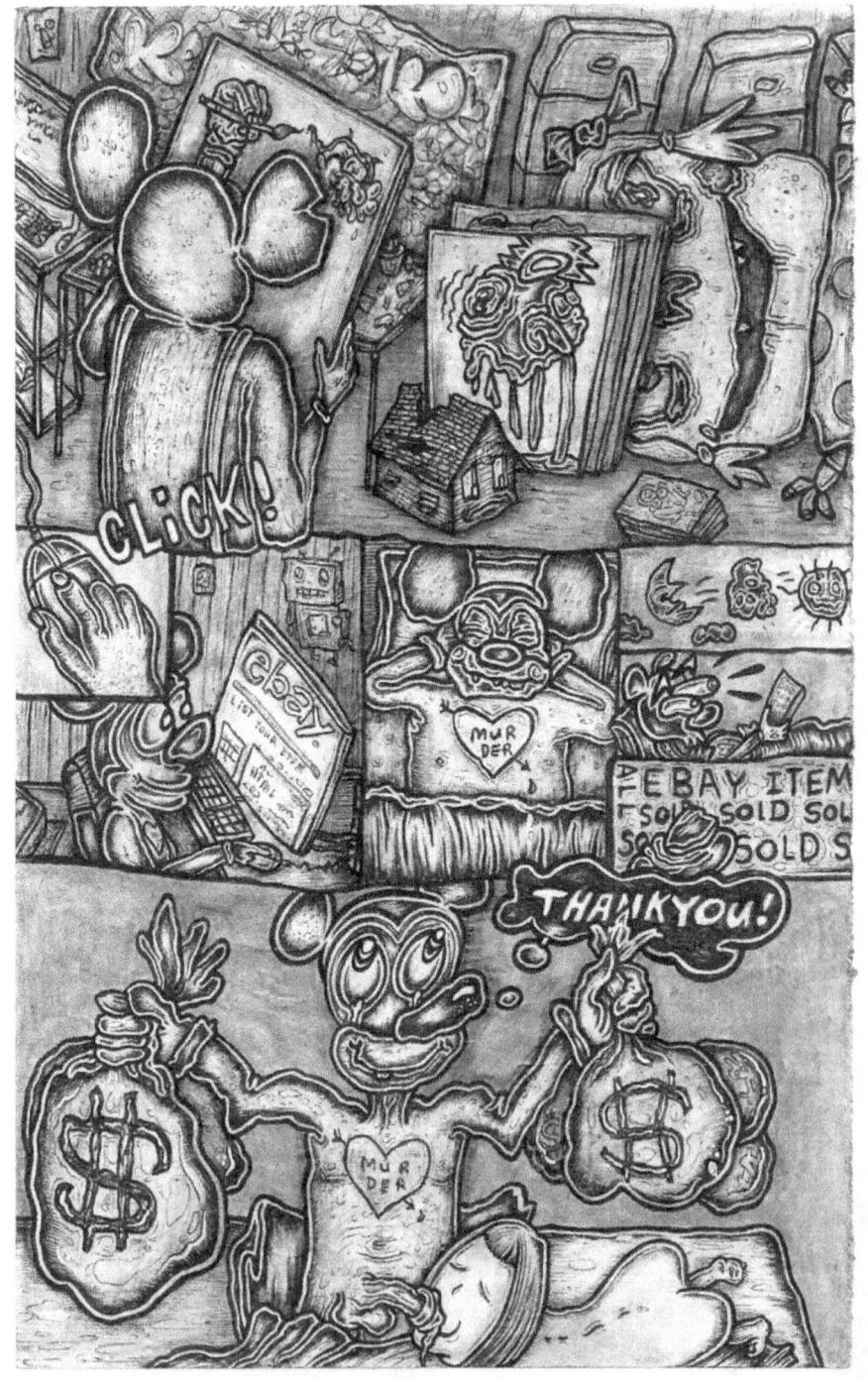

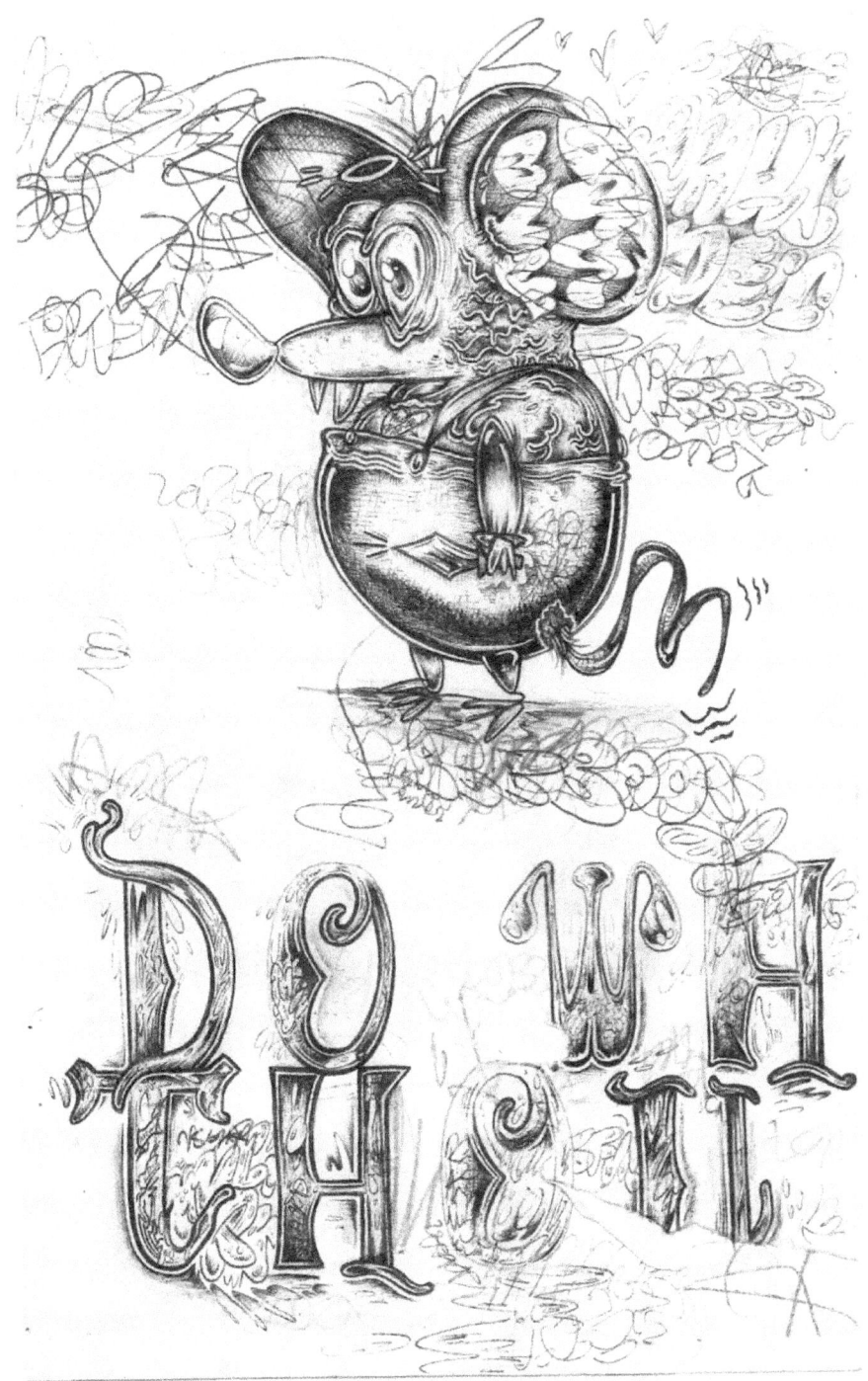

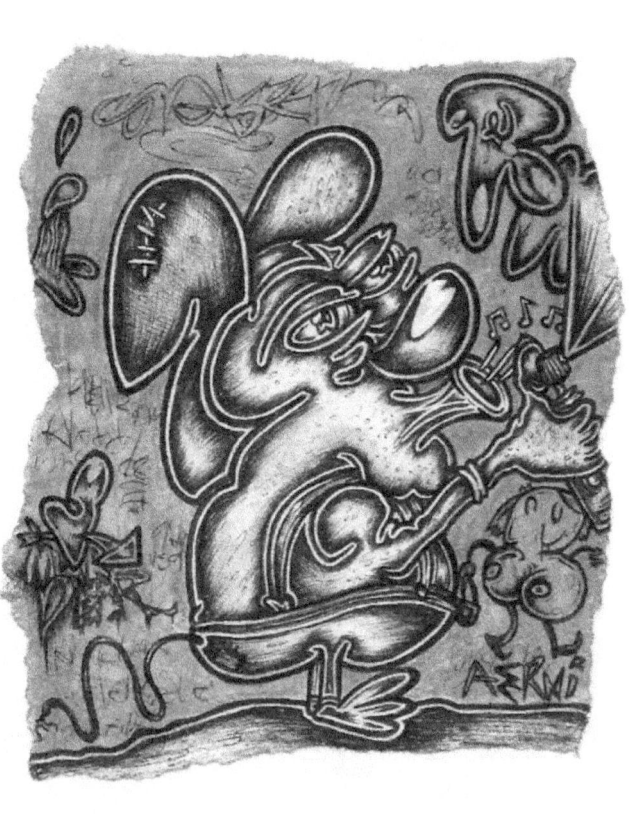

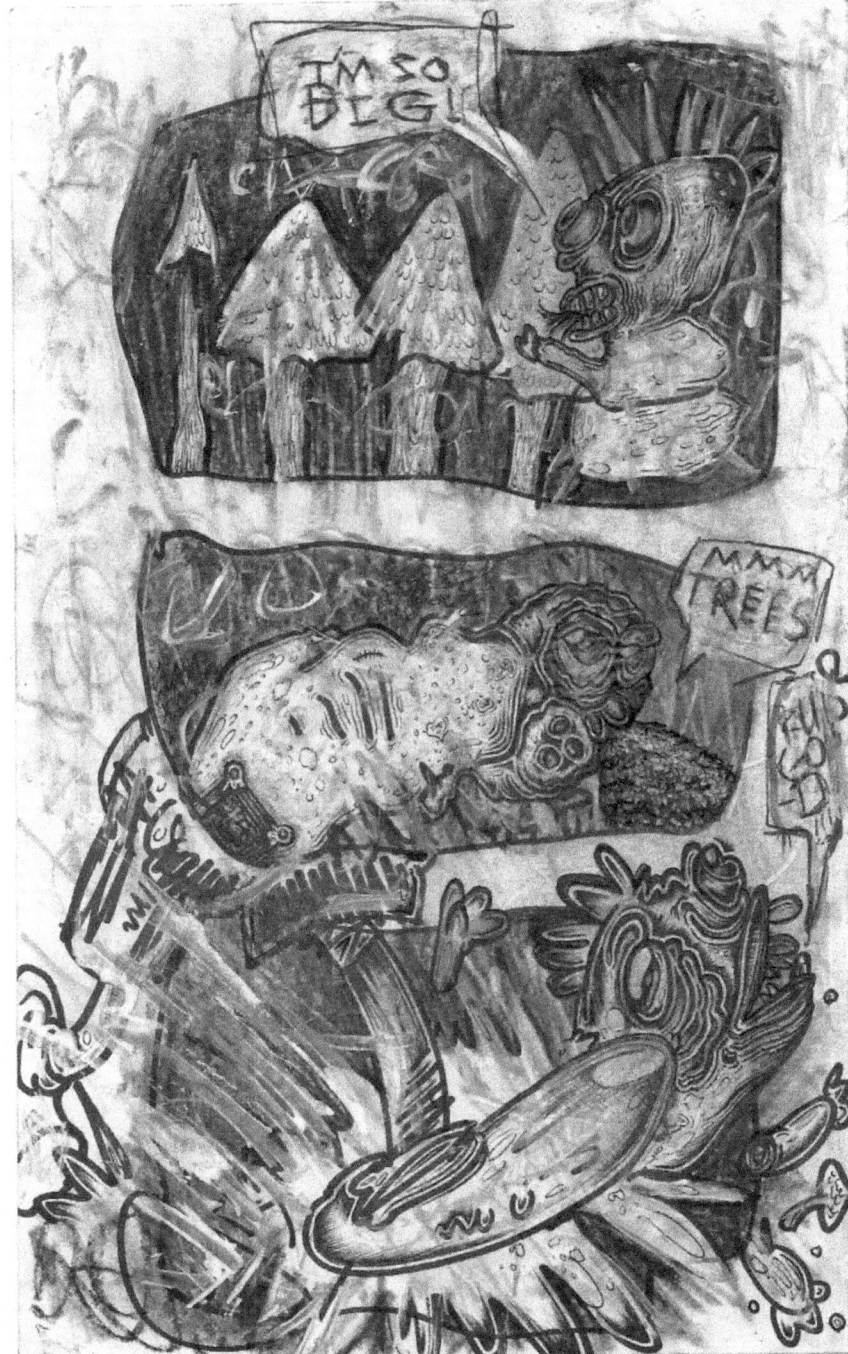

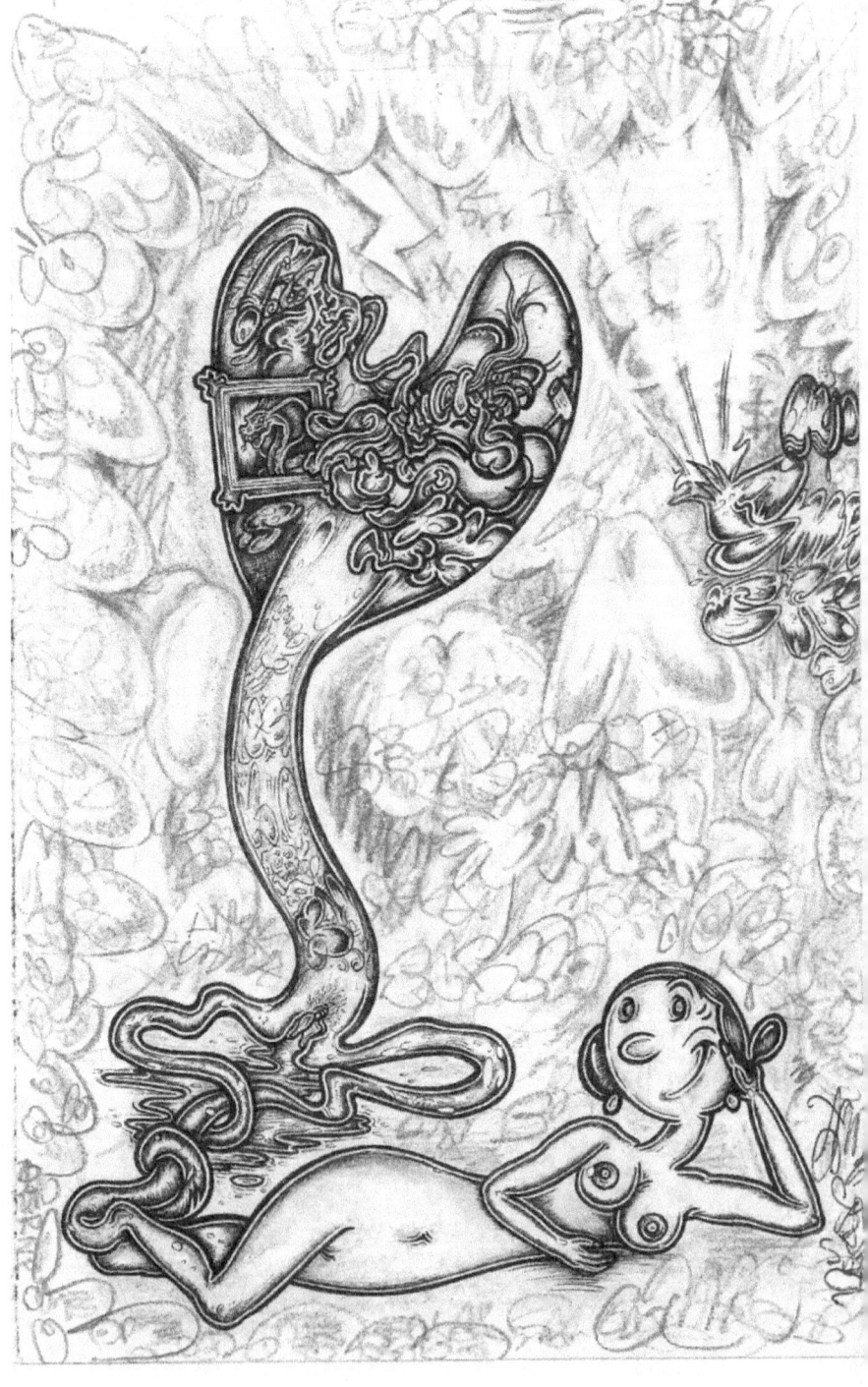

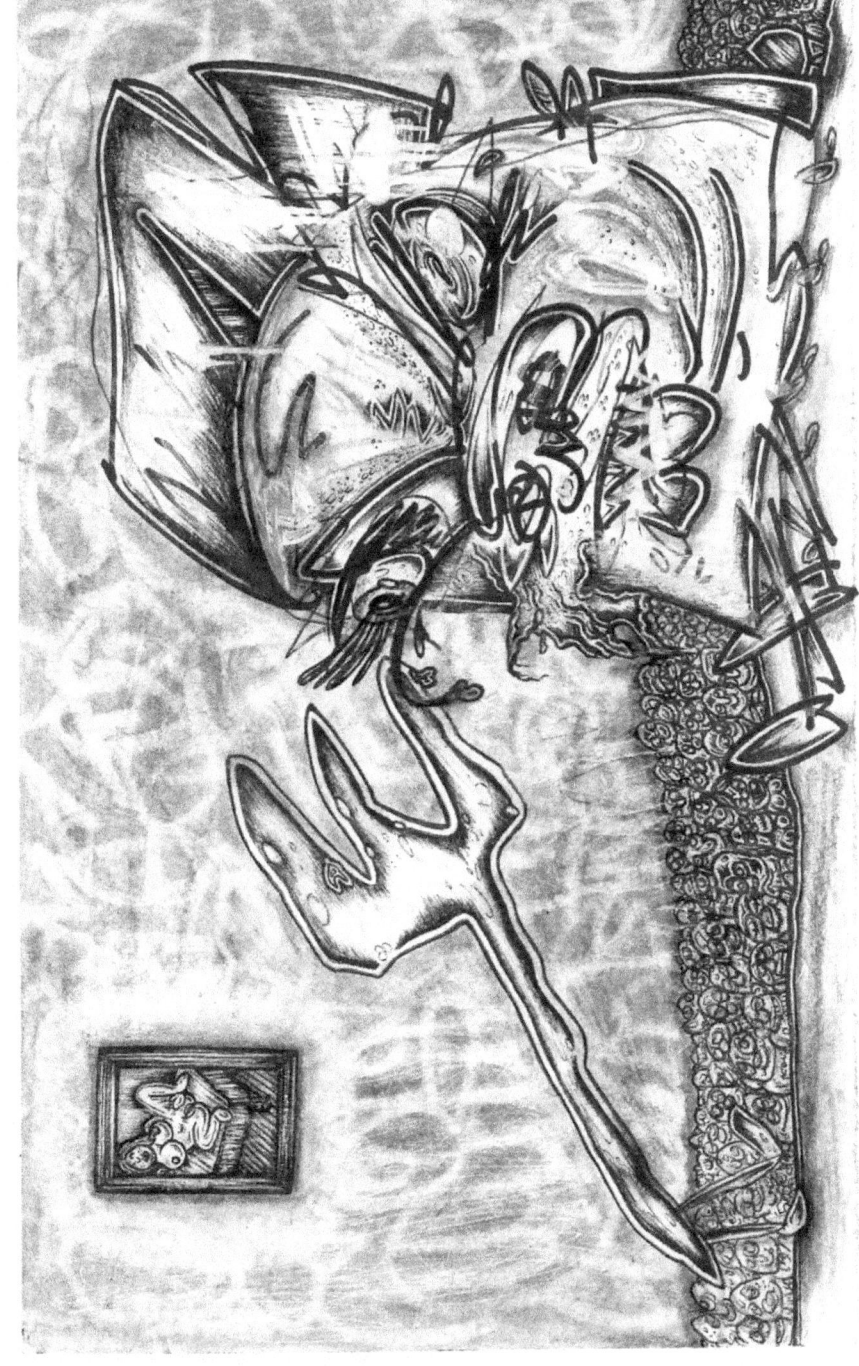

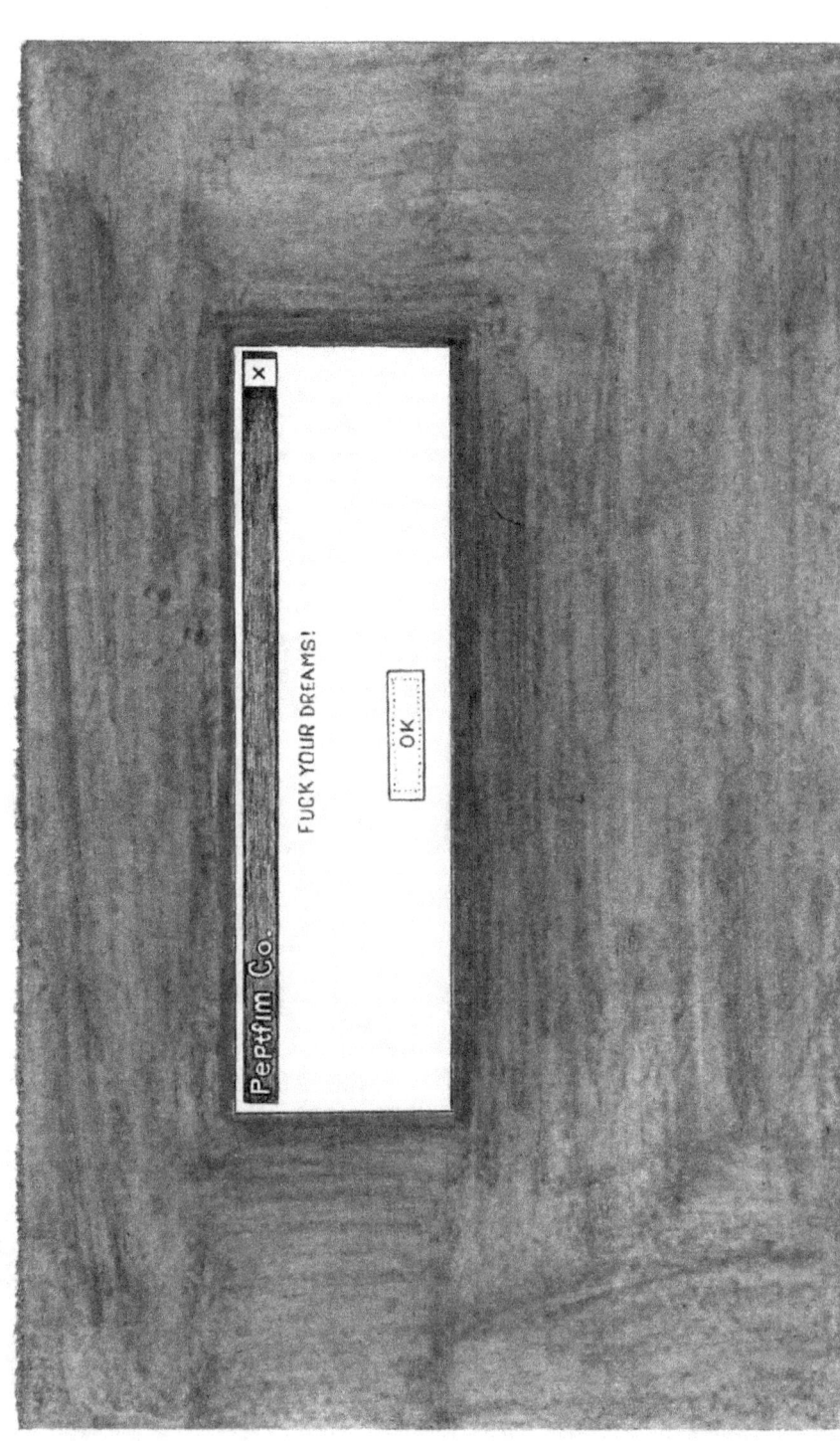

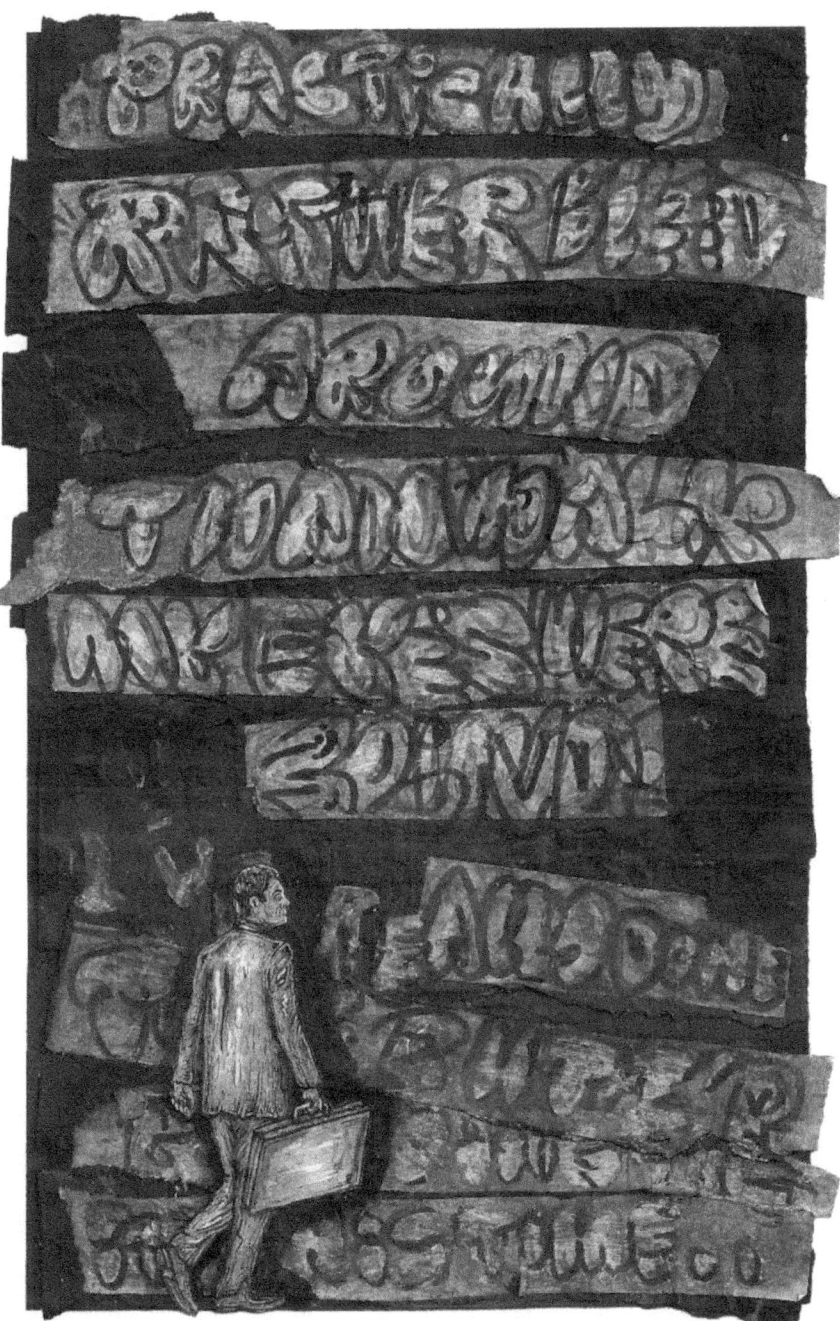

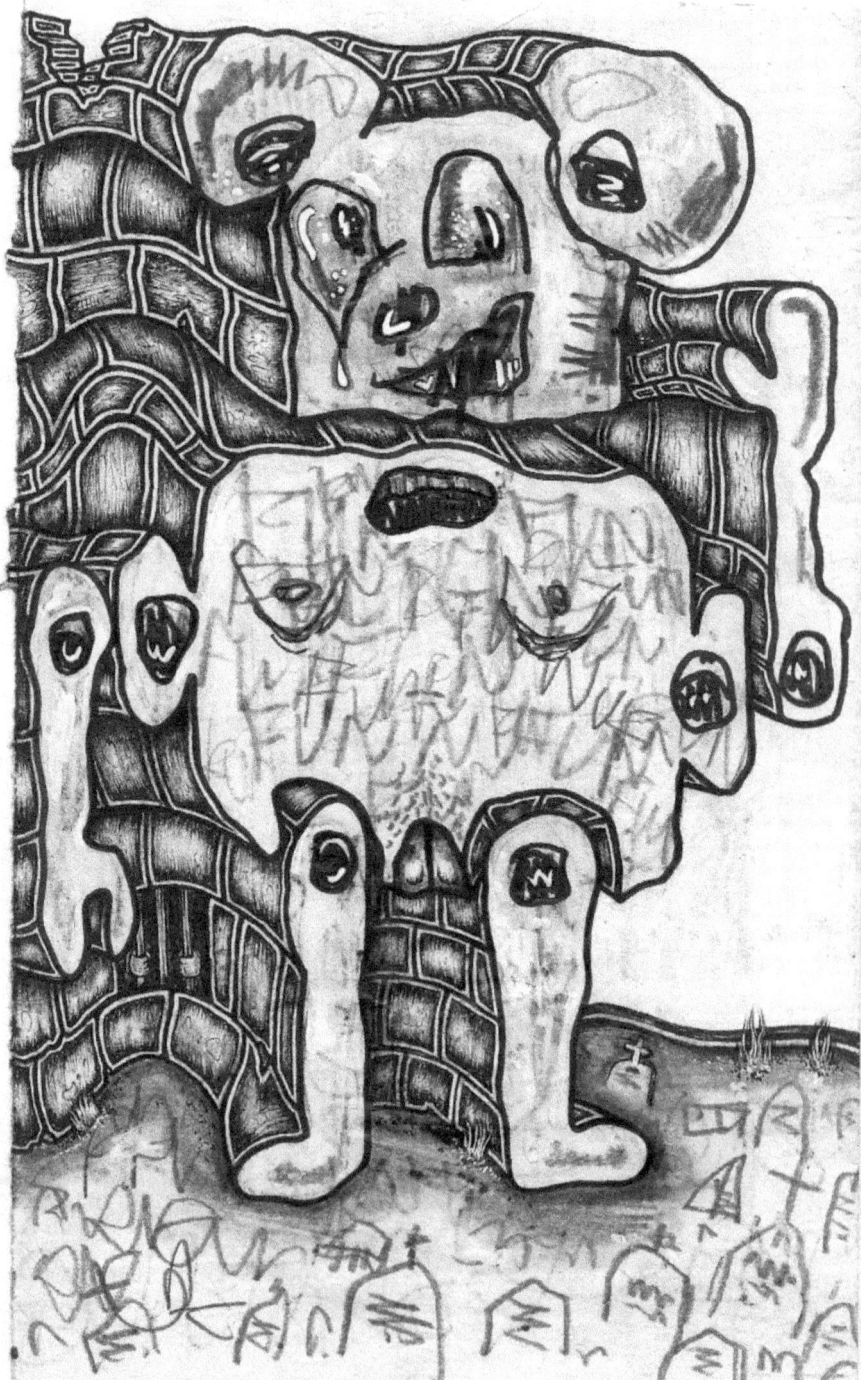

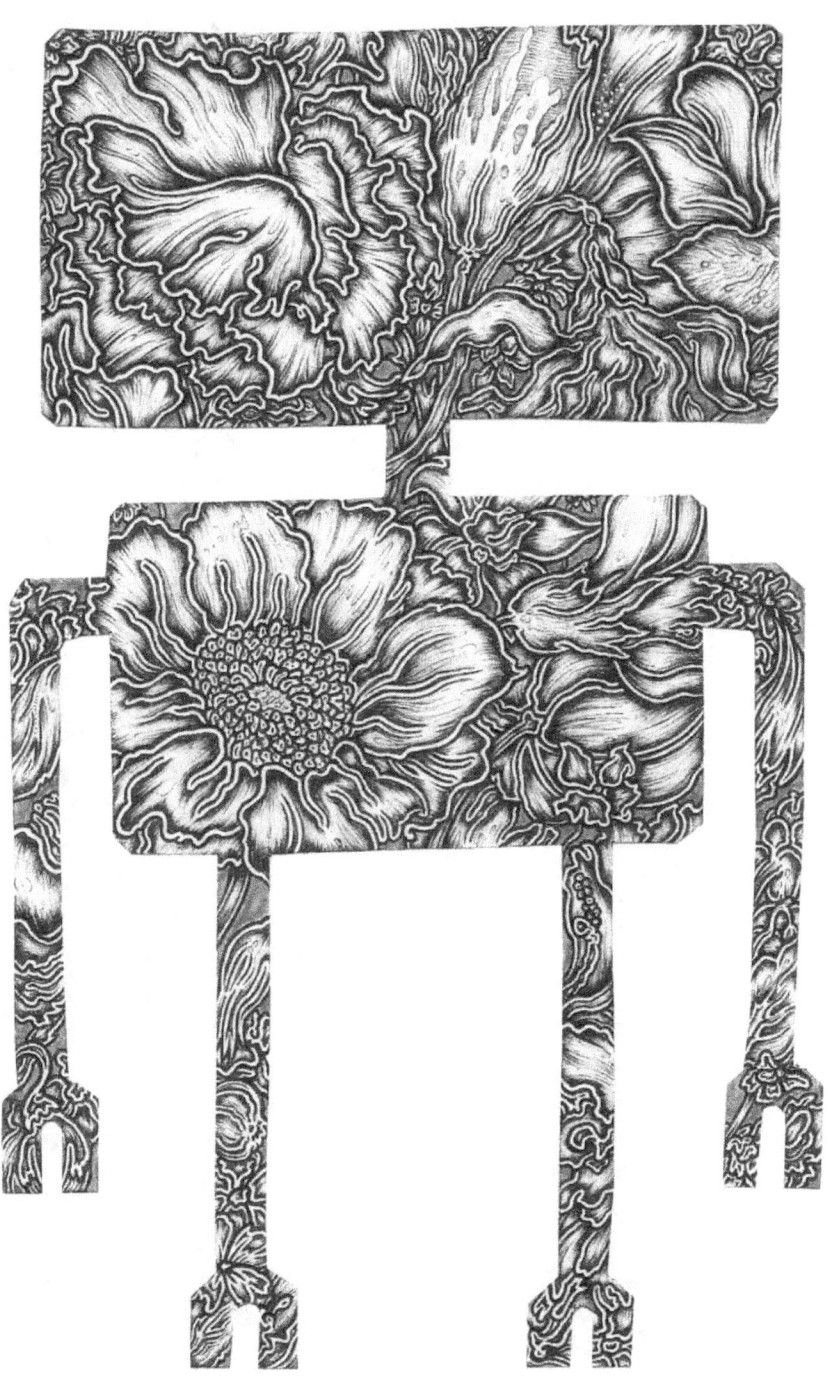

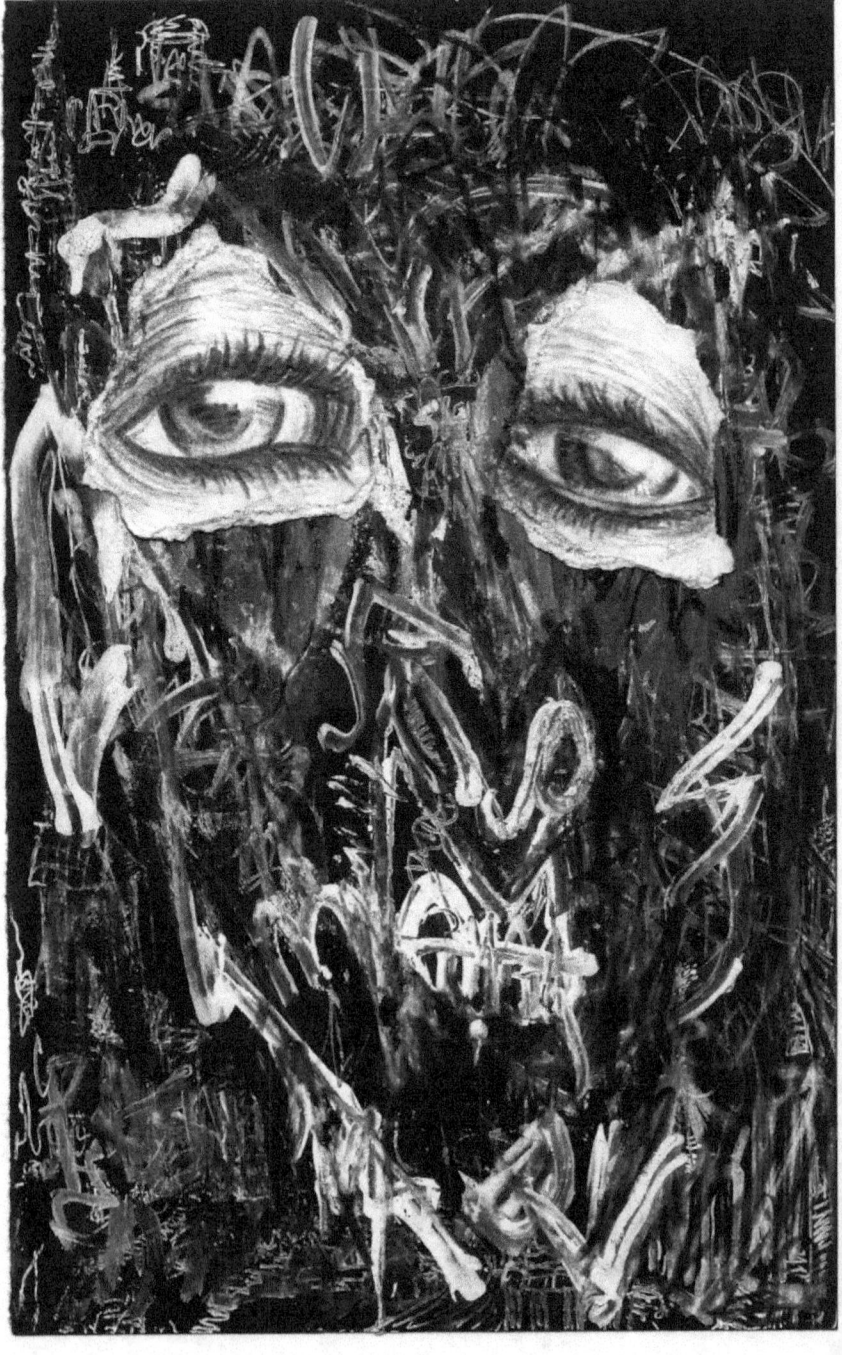

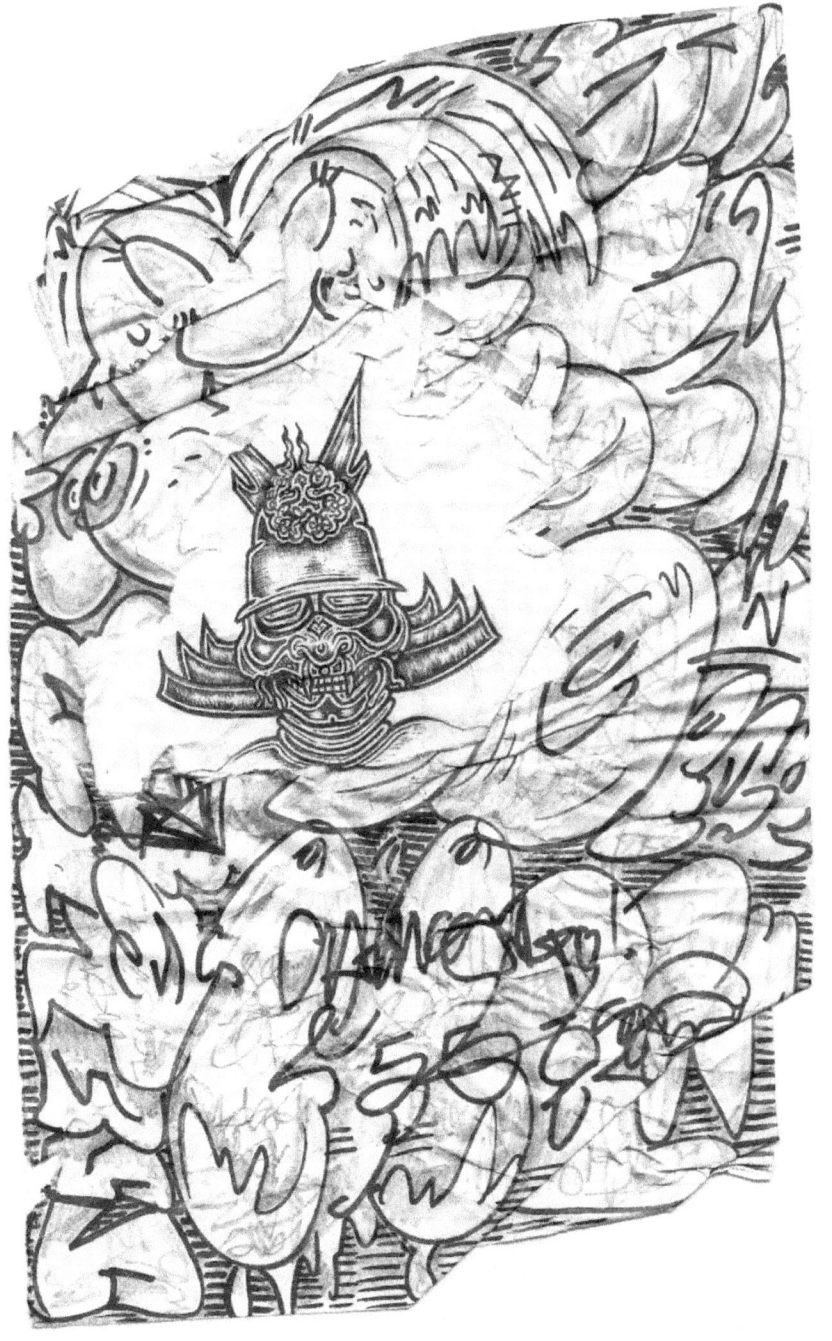

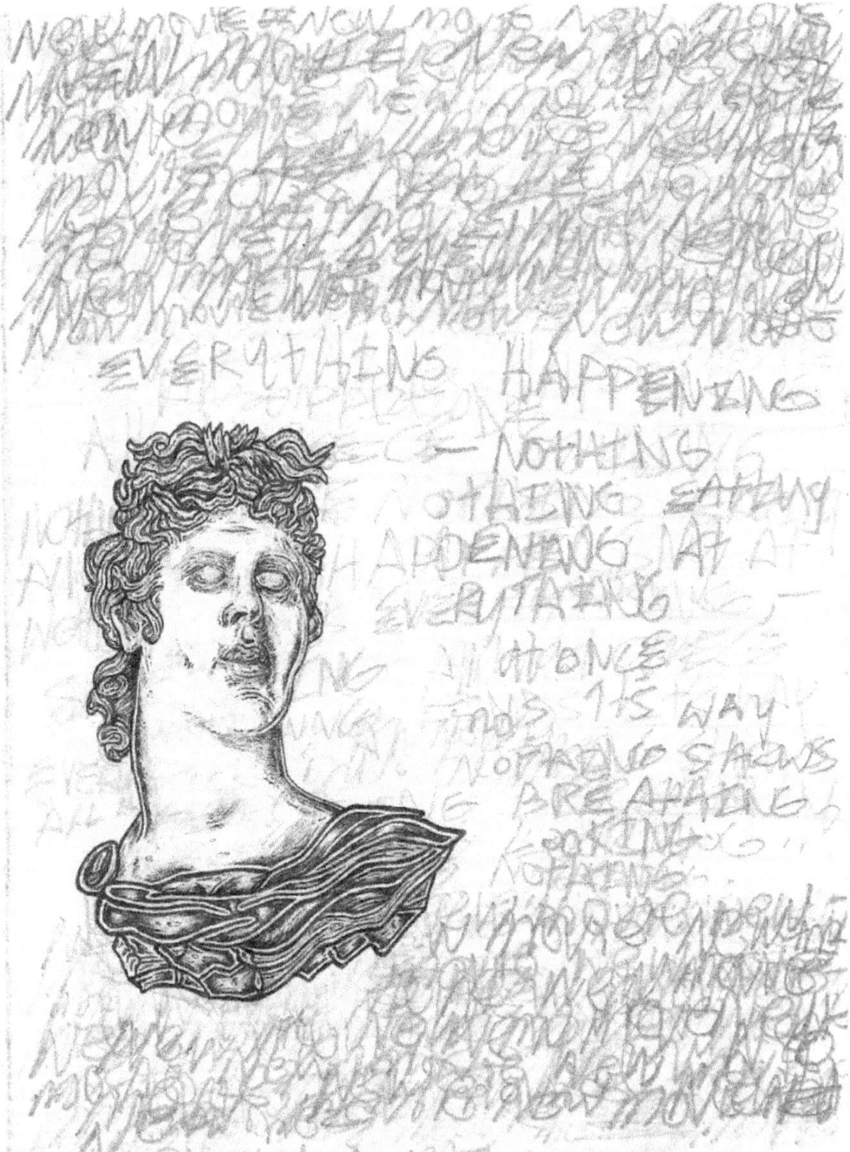

EVERYTHING HAPPENING
NOTHING
NOTHING EVERY
HAPPENING AT
EVERYTHING
ALL AT ONCE
FINDS ITS WAY
NOTHING STACKS
ARE A THING
LOOKING
NOTHING

BACK TO NOTHING ~ FRED RILEY
CHRIS, IDAN, ALL NOTHING
NOTHING NOTHING EVERY NOTHING
MATTERS. MATTERS.

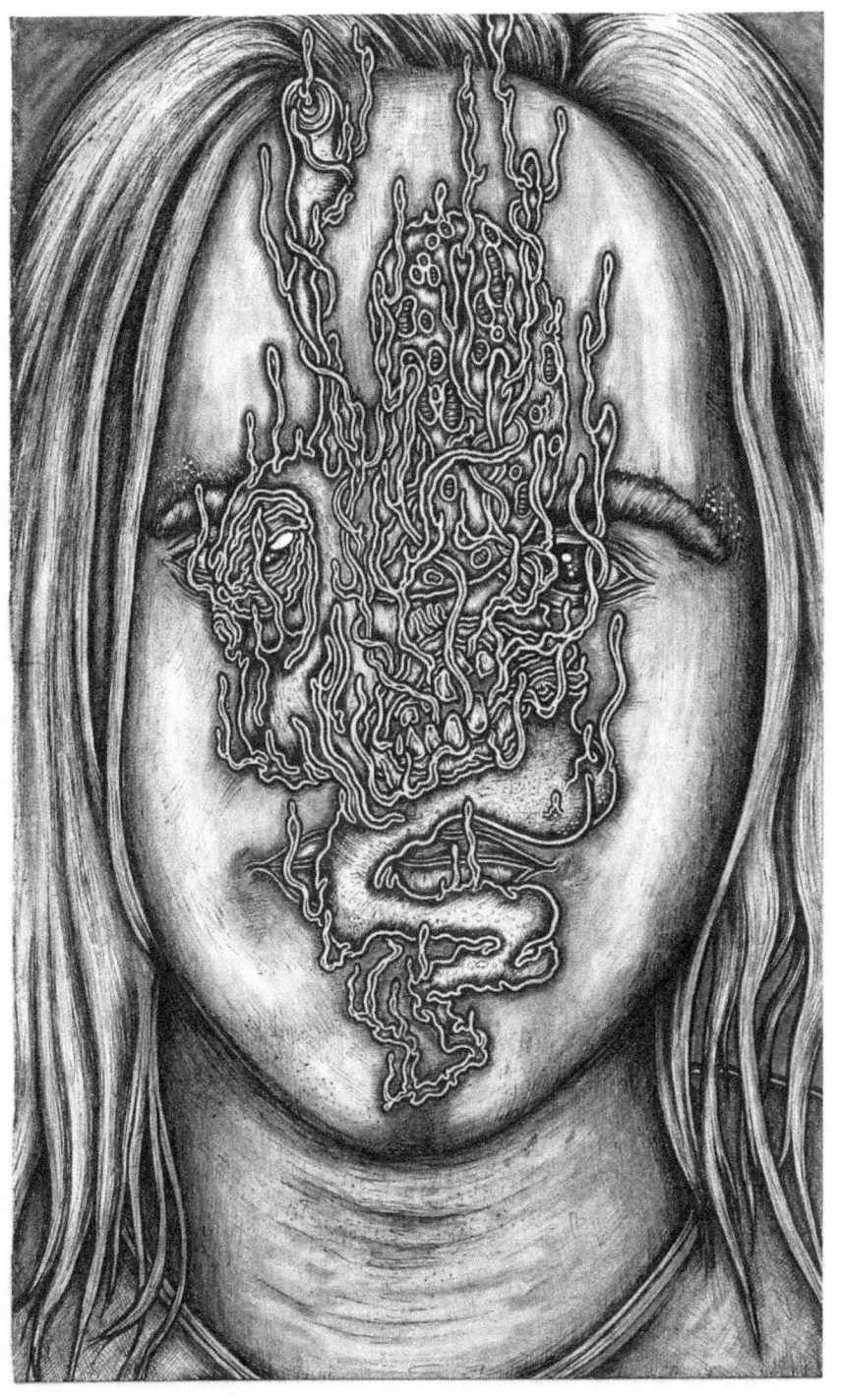

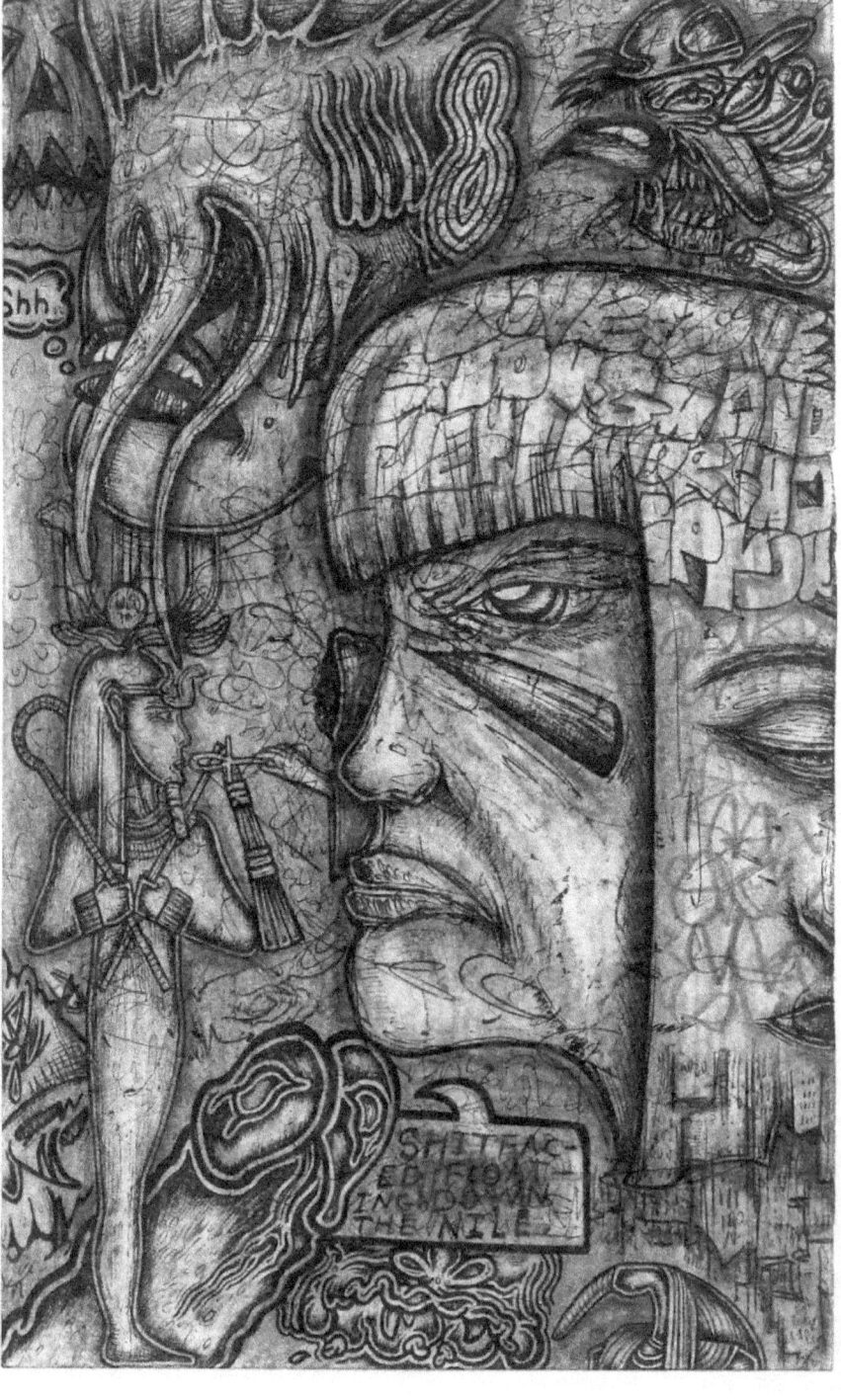

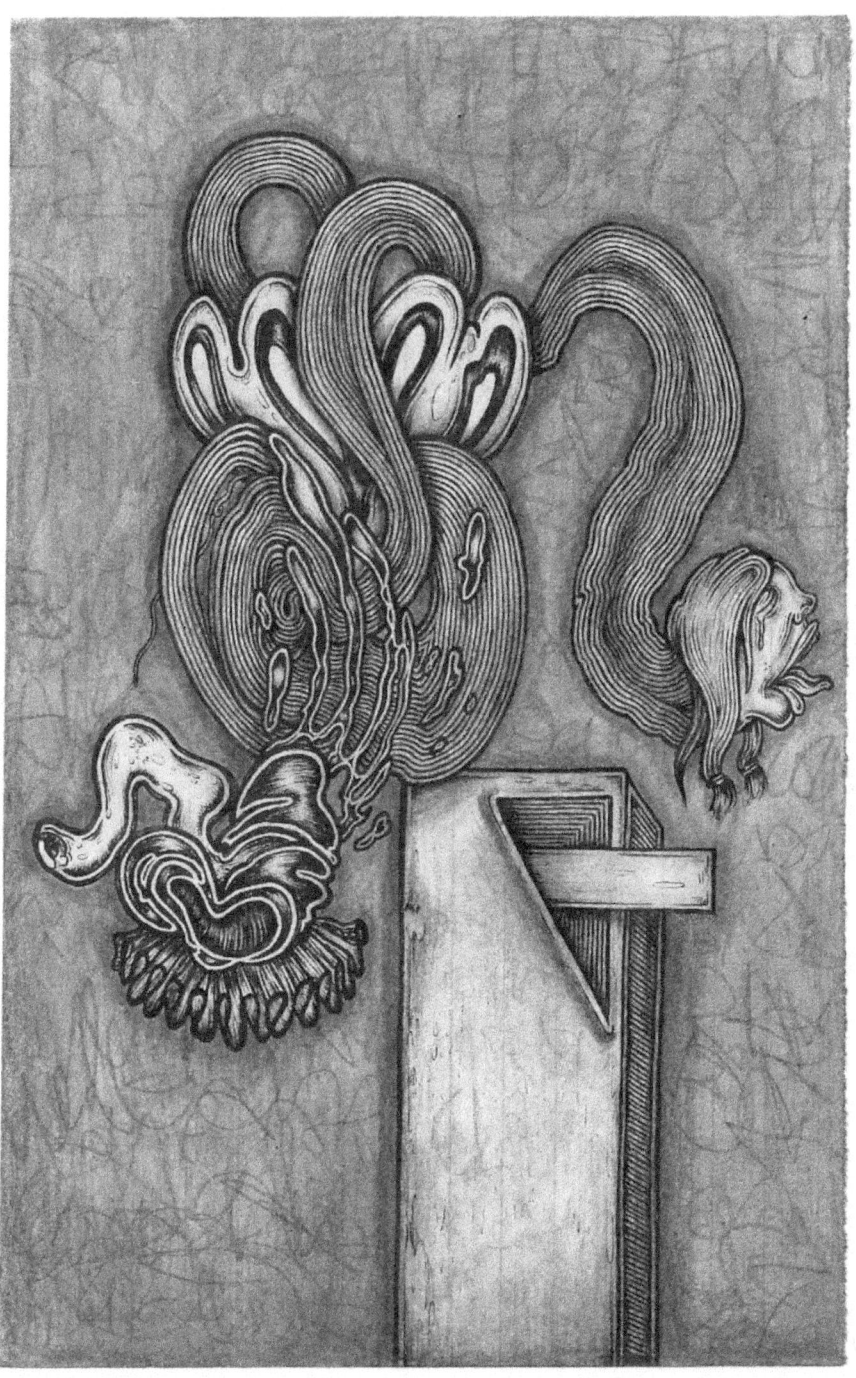

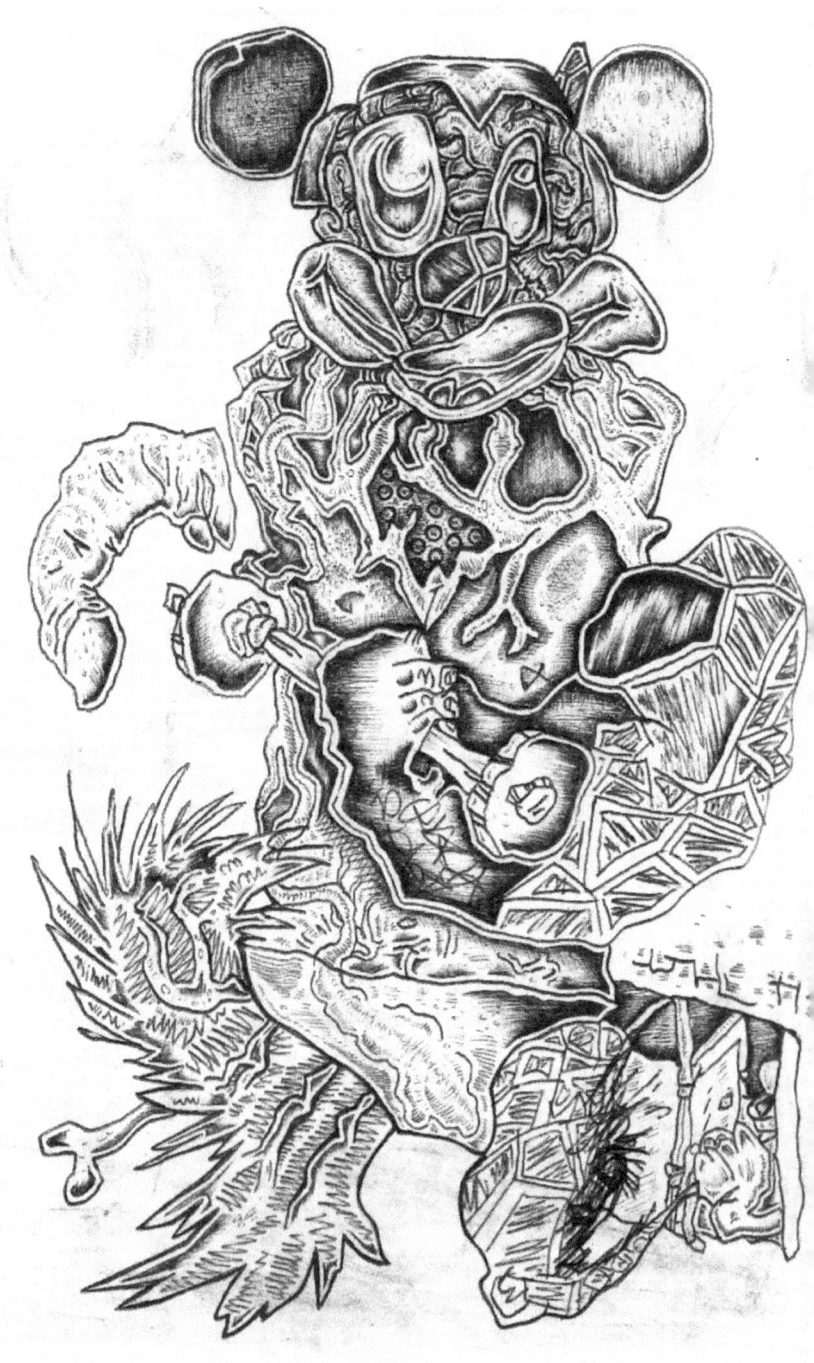

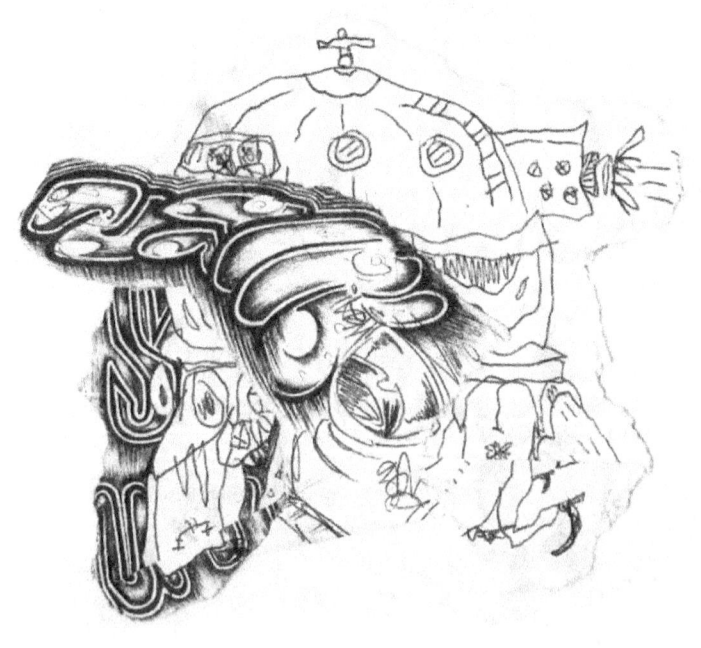

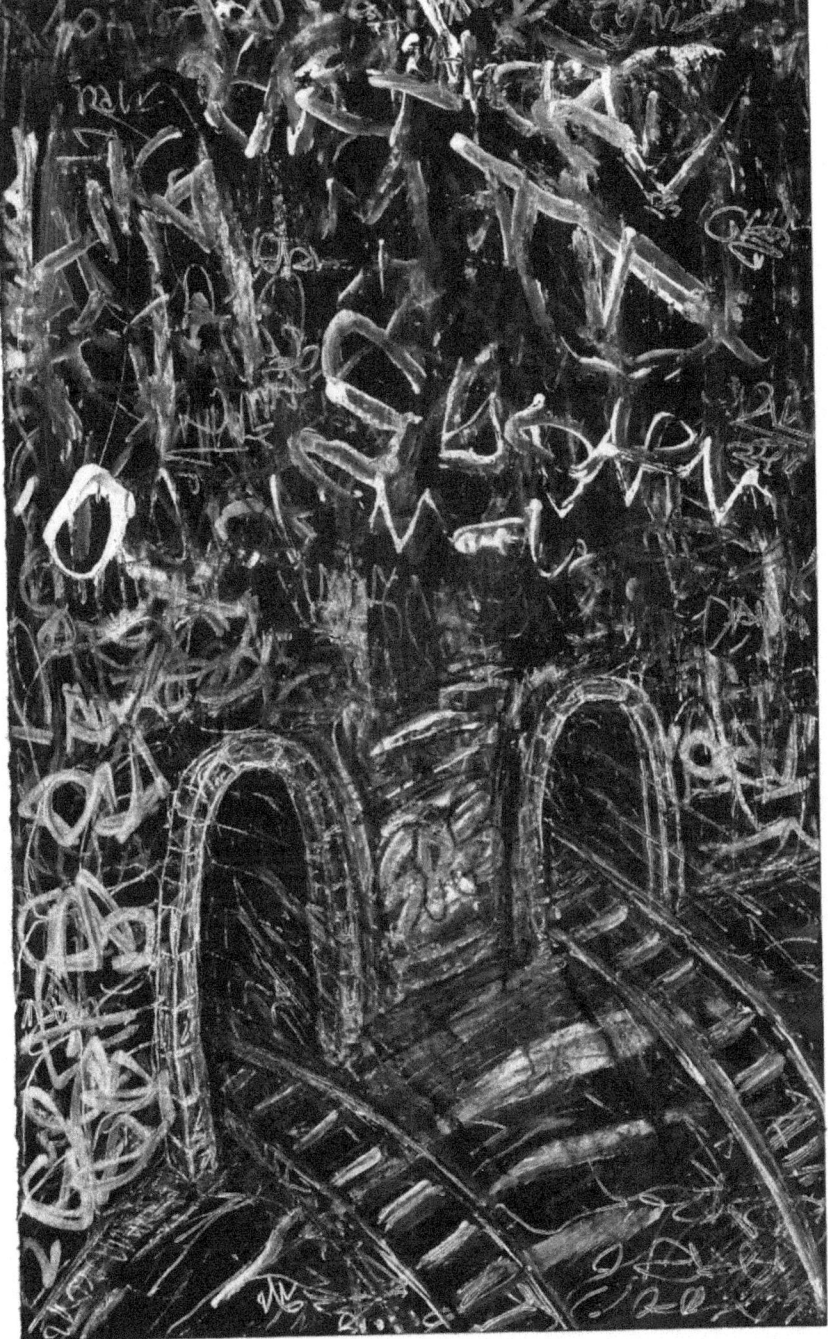

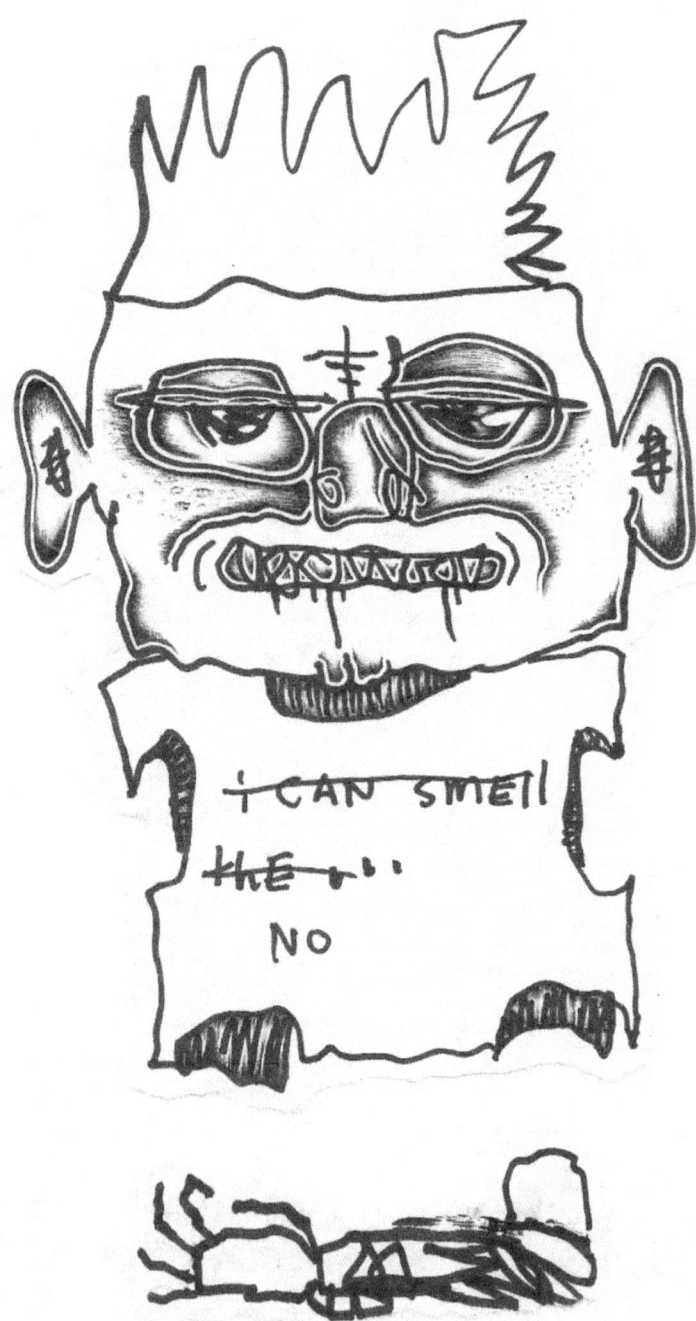

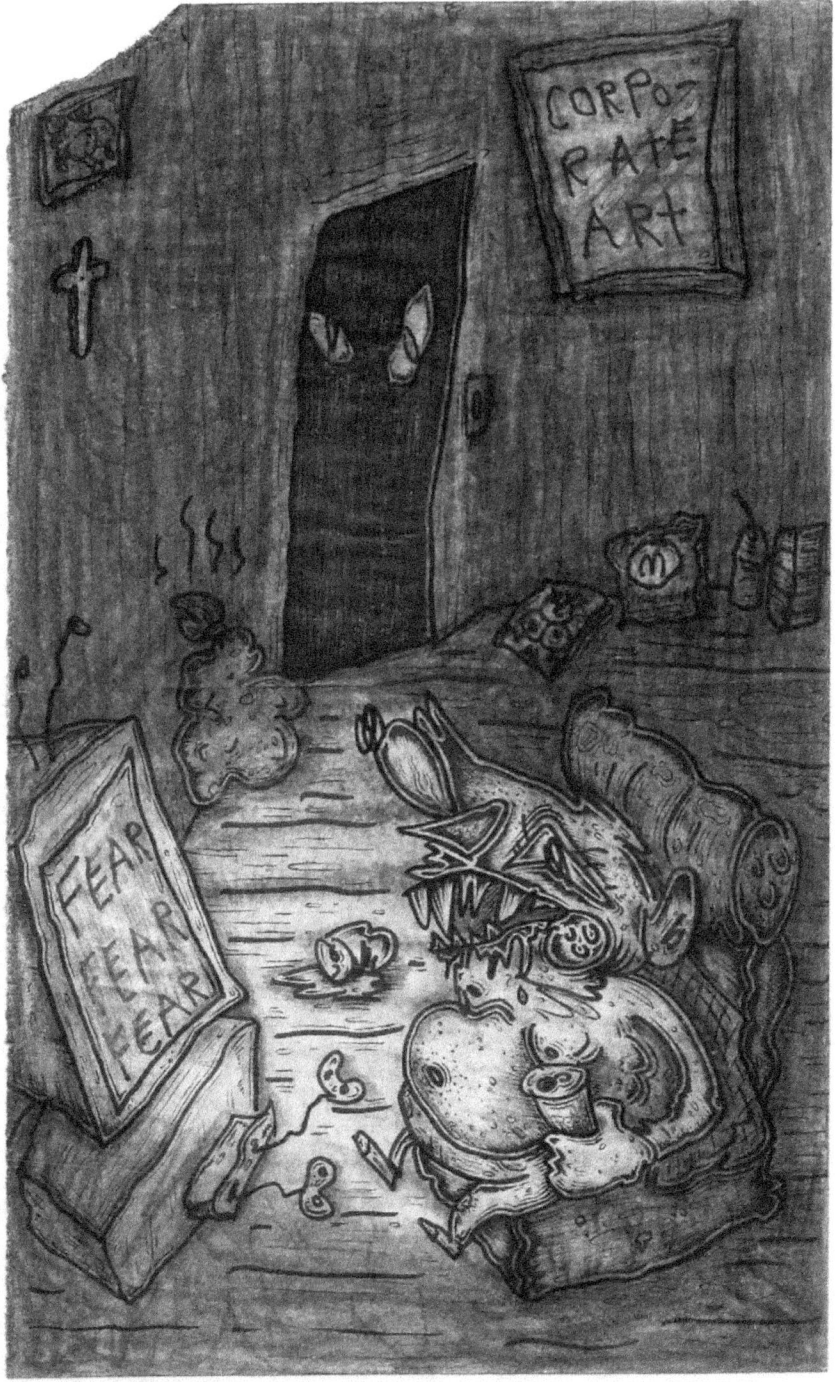

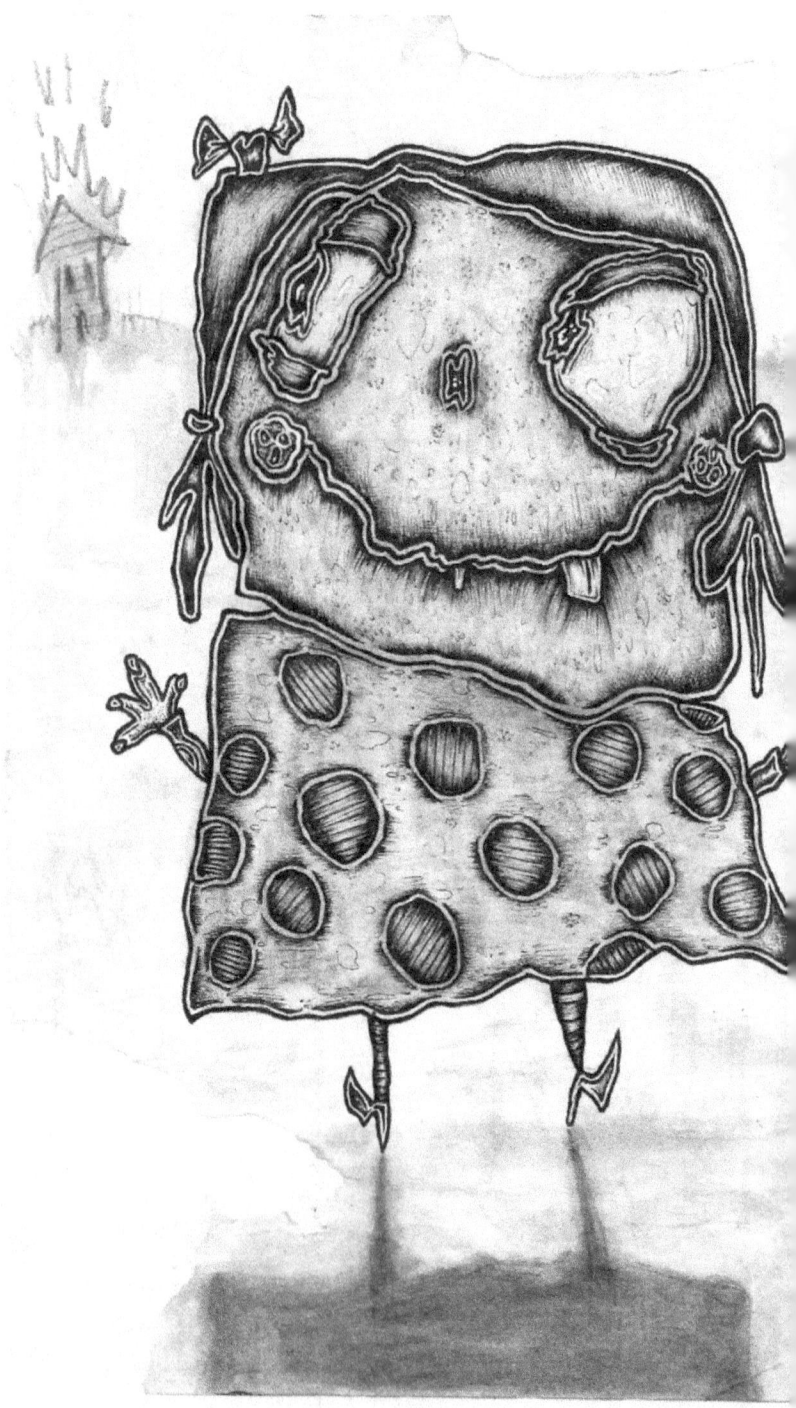

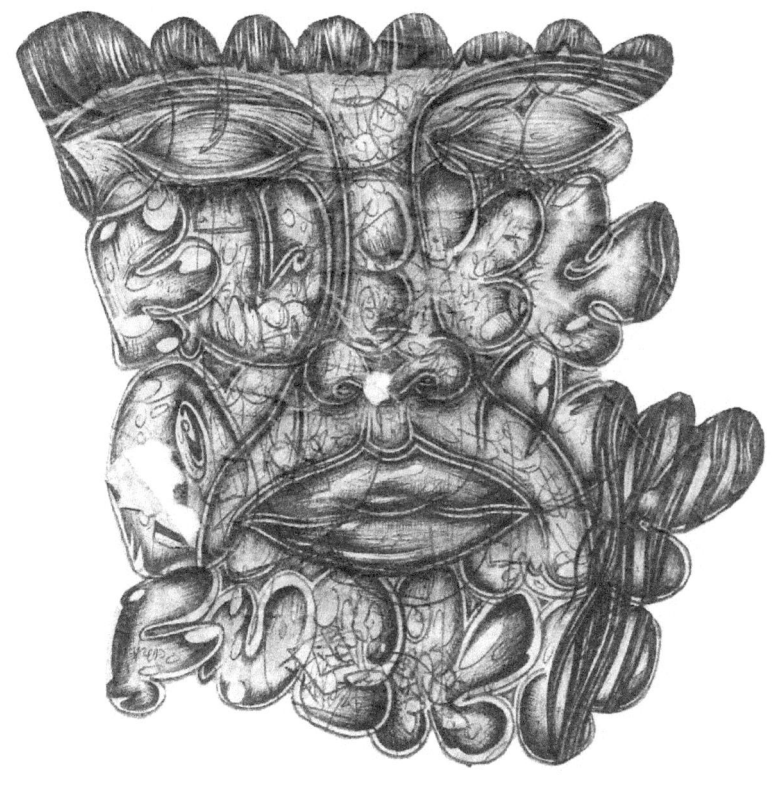

American painter, sculptor, author, photographer, and film maker, Justin Aerni, has garnered global attention for his thought- provoking artwork that combines satire and iconoclasm while examining the great enigmas of our time.

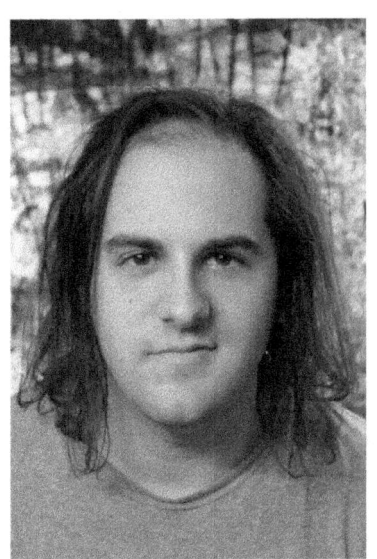

As popular as he is prolific, he has sold over 4,000 paintings worldwide within the past decade, and has written and illustrated eight books. - Erik Maell 2015

BIBLIOGRAPHY

2016 - Justin Aerni Sucks! (Book Of Original Drawings)
- ISBN-13: 978-1519180445 - Published August 2016.

2015 - American Trash (Photography) - ISBN-13: 978-1503293243
- Published January 2015.

2014 - Safari Into The Underworld (Choose Your Own Adventure Novel)
- ISBN-13: 978-1500365837 - Published July 2014.

2012 - Justin Aerni's Bitter Batter Brains (Poetry & Art)
- ISBN-13: 978-1479282906 - Published September 2012.

2011 - Bitter Batter Brains (Poetry & Art) - Published December 2011.

2011 - Damn Near Beautiful (Curated Outsider Art Book) - Published June 2011.

2009 - Dead Business Men (Graphic Novel) - ISBN-13: 978-1926617008
- Published April 2009.

2009 - Nonsense Relevant (Experimental Poetry & Art Book)
- Published March 2009.

2008 - Fighting For Fiction (Poetry & Digital Art Book) - Published August 2008.